SURPLUS UTILISATION IN AGRICULTURE

The Research Staff of the Project

Research Assistants

Amitava Chakravarty
Pradosh Nath
Nilay Mukherjee
Dabesh Bhowmik
Sankar Bhattacharjee

Field Investigators

Nirmal Kumar Das
Suchikkan Das
Sunil Sadhuka
Arun Kumar Ghosh
Debi Prasad Ghosh
Makhan Karmakar
Tapan Dasgupta

Office Assistant

Sumita Dutta

Surplus Utilisation in Agriculture
Study of a District in West Bengal

Ratan Khasnabis

Jyotiprakash Chakraborty

CONCEPT PUBLISHING COMPANY, NEW DELHI 110059

The Indian Council of Social Science Research (ICSSR) gave financial support towards the publication of this work. However, responsibility for the contents of the book - facts, opinions, conclusions, etc. - is entirely that of the authors and not of the ICSSR.

ISBN 81-7022-255-9

First Published 1989

Ratan **Khasnabis** (1946-)
Jyotiprakash **Chakraborty** (1944-)

Published by
Ashok Kumar Mittal
Concept Publishing Company
A 15-16, Commercial Block, Mohan garden
NEW DELHI-110059 (India)

Lesertypeset by
Microtech Advance Printing Systems (Pvt.) Ltd.
H-13, Bali Nagar,
NEW DELHI-110015

Printed in India by
A.P. Offset
Naveen Shahdara
DELHI-110032

ACKNOWLEDGMENTS

We gratefully acknowledge the financial support rendered by the Indian Council of Social Sciences Research for carrying out the field survey, the results of which are contained in this volume.

We owe a special debt to the Government officials of the Nadia District, particularly to Mr. Parimal Banerjee, the then S.D.O, Krishnanagar, without whose active help, it might not have been possible to conduct the field survey in a terrain which was not always hospitable.

In academic matters, we have incurred a long list of obligations during the years of work on the theme of surplus utillsation in agriculture. The foremost is, of course, that of Ashok Rudra of Visva-Bharati, who provided us with valuable criticism and advice that helped us shapess the ideas about many of the complex empirical and theoretical issues involved in this survey. Among other understanding and constructive critics, we must mention Arun Majumdar of Visva-Bharati, Nikhilesh Bhattacharjee and Ranjit Kumar Lahiri of the Indian Statistical Institute; Arup Mallick, Sankar Dhar, Anil Sarkar, Ashok Nag, Nabinananda Sen and Arabinda Bhattacharjee of Calcutta University; Amitava Sen of Kalyani University and Biswanath Santra of Bidhan Chandra Krishi Visvavidyalaya. Needless to say, none of them is responsible for the errors that may remain in this volume.

We would be lacking in gratitude if we fail to mention the labour of love rendered by Nirmalendu Nath right from the initiation to the final phase of the survey. His able assistance in quantitative analysis, particularly in heavy statistical work contained in many of the chapters, should be mentioned particularly.

We would also like to put on record the appreciation of the services of the field workers and the research staff who carried out the arduous field investigations and the most painstaking work of preparing a large number of summary tables. We feel that the output has been more than what was expected in terms of price efficiency, out of the paltry sum the project could afford to offer them. Indeed, most of them took up this work out of their eagerness to come into contact with the social reality in rural Bengal.

Thanks are also due to Krishna Raj, Editor, *The Economic and Political Weekly*, who was kind enough to publish an appendix chapter of this report in his esteemed journal.

CONTENTS

INTRODUCTION

I

In 1969, Ashok Rudra and two others examined some data related to a sample of big farmers of Punjab [32] and concluded that there were not very many farmers who could be treated as capitalist farmers [29]. Utsa Patnaik raised certain questions related to Rudra's methods [28] of studying capitalism. Rudra replied, Patnaik contested. Paresh Chattopadhyay entered into the debate with Althusser's Marxism [4]. And thus began the famous Indian debate on the mode of production in agriculture which is still continuing.

Contributing subsequently to the debate, Rudra submits that the debate in terms of certain modes of production' is merely pedantic; 'for purpose of practice, it is sufficient to have a correct class analysis - that is, correct characterisation of the different features, traits, relations of dominance, etc, of classes taken in their dynamic setting - whether or not one can conceive of all these things to constitute a mode of production of standard species, such as capitalism, feudalism, etc.'[30, p918]. In order to derive a correct class analysis, Rudra then considers certain characteristic distinctions between capitalist and pre-capitalist relations. 'One of the distinguishing characteristics of capitalist relations,' writes Rudra, 'is the accumulation of productive capital through re-investment of the surplus appropriated by the owners of the means of production' [ibid, p918]. This is a method of surplus-use which differs distinctly from that of the feudal appropriator who typically utilises the surplus for purposes of consumption. Inclusion of such a criterion alongwith others related to the method of surplus-generation is necessary because, according to Rudra, re-investment of surplus for productive purposes is not logically implied in the extraction of surplus through the process of purchasing labour power. Rudra cites from Marx's text[1] ' to establish his point.

Rudra's extreme position that the discussion on the 'mode of production' is absolutely unnecessary, might not be shared by many. However, Rudra is not alone to hold the view that the methods of surplus use are to be studied as well, for identifying the agrarian relations[2].

The position of Rudra and others has been criticised by Paresh Chattopadhyay [henceforth PC] who raises some crucial theoretical issues related to the debate on the mode of production. In the course of a brief review of the theoretical position as expounded in his two part contribution [4, 5] to the debate, PC reasserts [6] that capital is primarily not a thing but a relation., 'Capital' and 'capitalism' being equivalent, capitalism implies a single relation, 'the relation between the direct producers and their conditions of production, which, becoming independent of them, and passing under the control of the non-producers, confront them and dominate them as capital' [6,

---

1. 'Capitalist production is distinguished from the outset by two characteristic features. First, it produces its products as commodities. The fact that it produces commodities does not differentiate it from other modes of production, but rather the fact that being a commodity is the dominant and determining characteristic of its products. This implies, first and foremost, that the labour himself comes forward merely as a seller of commodities, and thus as a free wage-labourer, so that labour appears in general as wage-labour. The second distinctive feature of the capitalist mode of production is the production of surplus value as the direct aim and determining motive of production. Capital produces essentially capital and does so only to the extent it produces surplus value. Production for value and surplus value implies, as has been shown in the course of our analysis, the constantly operating tendency to reduce the labour time necessary for the production of a commodity, i.e. its value, below the actually prevailing social average. The pressure to reduce cost price to its minimum becomes the strongest lever for raising the social productiveness of labour, which, however, appears here only as a continual increase in the productiveness of capital'[23, p263].

2. For example, see [1], [33], [8]. Utsa Patnaik's [26] position is rather ambivalent. She gives in to Chottopadhayay's equation of generalised commodity production with wage labour. At the same time, she maintains that a separate criterion based on re-investment of surplus is called for under the 'highly specific conditions of stagnation under colonial exploitation' due to which 'the destitute peasants turned labourers do not constitute free labourers as under capitalism'.

A86]. Such a single relation is expressed through wage labour. The extent of development of wage labour is, therefore, the indicator of capitalism. All other features of capitalism including the productive recycling of surplus in the form of extended reproduction, are logically implied by the single relation of wage labour. Therefore, they need not be studied separately. PC cites Lenin [11, p437] and Marx in volume II of Capital [22, p512] to establish his point. He also tries to counter the opposite opinion, developed on the basis of a quotation from volume III of Capital [see foot note 1], by suitably utilising Marx's text to show that 'Marx's first feature - that is generalised commodity production including labour power as a commodity - already determines the whole character of the capitalist mode of production and the second feature follows from the first' [6, p A-86].

While there is little dispute on the point that capital is primarily a relation, we are in disagreement with PC as regards the interpretation of this relation. The essence of this relation is of course that the possessor of means of production and subsistence and the possessor of nothing but labour-power must confront each other as buyer and seller. But this is not sufficient. Any confrontation of this nature does not imply capitalism[3]. A confrontation of this nature becomes capitalism only when such buying of labour power is done for the production of exchange value and thereby for surplus value. By interpreting the capitalist relation in terms of an indicator related to the labour market alone, one might miss this essential ingredient that describes the relation itself. However, PC seems to be aware of this difficulty. While using the category of 'labour power as commodity'

3. Free purchase and sale of labour might be associated with pre-capitalism as well. In fact, such a phenomenon was present in ancient Rome (PC has quoted from Marx to recognise this point) and Europe in general before the bourgeois order had set in. But these were not associated with capitalism. PC quoted from Marx to show that such sales were not related to commodity production, and therefore the labour did not assume the form of wage labour. PC missed a very important point in this context. Even if such sales and purchases of labour were organised for producing commodities, the sale & purchase would not have assumed wage form. It would have assumed wage form only within the framework of generalised commodity production which has productive recycling of surplus as one of its features. As if to remind this condition, Marx, while describing such a free sale of labour under precapitalism considers a situation where free labour produced not use value but exchange value and notes 'the free workers produced value for him [i.e., the nobility Authors] but then only in relation to the superfluity, *in order to increase superfluous luxury consumption*', [24, p13, emphasis added] i.e. not to augment capital as the productive recycling implies

as the indicator of capitalism, he is cautious enough to 'firmly place it within the frame work of generalised commodity production' [6, P A-87] so that the act of buying the labour power could necessarily imply creation of exchange value.

Had he been a bit less dogmatic, PC might have realised that by introducing, quite correctly, such an additional condition [in the form of the existence of generalised commodity production], he had to have recourse to categories outside the labour market. A generalised commodity production is not synonymous to conditions necessary for the existence of 'labour power as commodity'. It includes some other features also. This, we submit, is not recognised by PC who seems to have mistaken by equating generalised commodity production with wage labour. Now, a necessary condition for the existence of generalised commodity production [which implies buying of labour power for the purpose of creation of exchange value] is the extended reproduction implying re-investment of surplus value, or the 'transformation of surplus value into capital'. This is not included in the study of capitalism that could be developed on the basis of the single indicator related to the labour market alone.

The inclusion of the feature of extended reproduction has a significant implication in the relational plane. It qualifies the act of buying of labour power in such a way that the act of confrontation and domination of the conditions of production assumes a special character. Given extended reproduction, labour power becomes purchasable so far as it preserves the means of production in their capacity of capital, reproduces its cwn value as capital and yields in unpaid labour a source of additional capital[4]. Thus even when capital is introduced as a relation, the study of the mode of surplus use remains relevant.

One might dodge all these by introducing an omnibus conceptual category called 'wage labour'. Wage labour is defined as the free sale of labour power under the generalised commodity production, which, in its turn, implies a situation when products have already assumed value forms, the expanded reproduction being a necessary concomitant to that. Formally, there is nothing wrong if one intro-

---

4. Thus, the conditions of sale and purchase of labour power or the nature of confrontation between owners of labour and owners of means of production become different from what it was during medieval period.

duces an omnibus term which includes all the crucial features of capitalism. But the extension of the logic to hold that the re-investment of surplus value and the accumulation of capital are *derived* from the single relation of wage labour and hence they are not to be studied separately is fallacious. They are not derived from the single relation called wage labour; they very much describe the generalised commodity production, as the wage labour does.

The protagonists of the view that the 'single relation described through wage-laboure is sufficient to describe capitalism' seem to be unaware of the fact that from the same logic of introducing a 'catch all' term, the extended reproduction could very much be introduced as a *sine qua non* of capitalism. An extended reproduction, implying transformation of surplus value into capital, includes, *inter alia,* creation of value and hence buying [and therefore selling] of labour power at its value within the ambit of its connotation and thus a separate study on the buying and selling of labour power might be considered redundant[5].

PC quotes Lenin and then Marx in order to defend his position. Our submission is that such quotations do not help one understand the features of capitalism. The relevant quotations [11, p417] [22, p512] as explained by Lenin in a footnote, 'only refer to the *relation between commodity and capitalist production* [11, p437, emphasis added], and not to the concept of capitalism as such, as PC's interpretation suggests. The above quotations simply imply that capitalist production differs from commodity production of lower stages by virtue of its being commodity production of a higher stage when labour power has become a commodity. It only intends to describe this much. The features of this commodity production of the higher stage are never described unless one adds the following passage from Marx : 'labour power is sold today, not with a view to satisfying, by its service or by its product, the personal needs of the buyer. His aim is augmentation of his capital, production of commodities containing more labour than he pays for, containing therefore, a portion of value that costs him nothing; and that is nevertheless realised

---

5. PC quotes from Marx to show that extended reproduction as such does not imply accumulation of capital and therefore, it is not a *sine qua non* for capitalism. The quotation is rather misleading as such, the sale and purchase of labour is not also capitalism. Both of them indicates capitalism under generalised commodity production. PC's mistake, we submit, lies in equating generalized commodity production with wage labour.

when the commodities are sold. Production of surplus value is the absolute law of this mode of production. Labour power is only saleable so far as it preserves the means of production in their capacity of capital, reproduces its own value as capital, and yields in unpaid labour a source of additional capital. The condition of its sale, whether more or less favourable to the labourer, includes therefore the necessity of its constant reselling, and the *constantly extended reproduction of all wealth in the shape of capital*'. [20, p618-619, emphasis added]. Placed in this way, we find that extended reproduction is not a derived criterion as PC suggests, it is one of the conditions of the sale and purchase of labour power with a view to augmentation of capital, i.e., it is one of the conditions for the existence of wage labour.

Our submission is that the genesis of PC's fallacious approach in the non-recognition of the fact that although capital is a relation, it is 'not a simple relation, but a *process* in whose various moments, it is always capital' [24, p253]. The various moments of the process are described through the dialectical interaction in the form of struggle and unity of two aspects of the matter under study. In case of capital, this is described, through the unity and struggle of two elements, namely production and circulation[6]. 'Total production process of capital includes both the circulation process proper and the actual production process. These form the two great sections of its movement, which appears as the totality of these two processes'. [24, p620]. The link between these two aspects is provided by the feature of extended reproduction which is the consequence of relentless pursuit of profit on the part of the capitalists. While describing capital, such an aspect is to be taken care of. PC's approach, according to our understanding, does not incorporate this and hence it misses the dialectical essence of capital.

We are, therefore, in disagreement with PC and hold that a mode of production is described very much as a combination of the mode of surplus generation and its utilisation. 'Every society has a characteristic feature of surplus generation and its utilisation. The

---

6. It should be noted that this is exactly how Marx conceived capital. This is reflected through the scheme of Marx's study on Capital. Volume I of 'Capital' is entitled 'The Process of Capitalist Production; Volume II is 'the process of circulation of Capital'. These two aspects are united in volume III that described 'Capitalist Production as a whole'.

utilisation process differs corresponding to every society just as the generation process differs. The feudal appropriator typically utilises the surplus for the purpose of consumption. In the case of feudal lord, the surplus supported his excesses in luxury. The capitalist appropriator, on the other hand, typically utilises the surplus for re-investment with a view to expanding reproduction which, of course, is only a means to the end of continuously expanding the volume of profit. The typical pattern of capitalist production is ever expanding reproduction - the consequence of relentless pursuit of profit' [30,p318].

The study on the mode of surplus use becomes particularly significant when one considers a situation called 'semi-feudalism'. The term 'semi-feudal' is often used to describe a transitional situation where there is obvious and marked decline of a feudal natural economy alongwith a more or less retention of feudal forms of exploitation. The logical destiny of such a society is capitalism. The process of development of capitalism in such a society is that the feudal property is transformed into such economic forms that correspond to the requirements of the capitalist mode of production; labour then comes into the formal subordination of capital, i.e., a formal subsumption of labour under capital is attained. Capital revolutionises production techniques so that subsequently there appears a real subsumption of labour. The society is then[7] transformed into a capitalist society.

---

7. 'With the real subsumption of labour under capital a *complete* (and constantly repeated) revolution takes place in the mode of production, the productivity of the workers and *in the relations between workers and capitalists* [21, p1035, emphasis added]. Marx also writes, (with real subsumption) 'capitalist production now establishes itself as a mode of production *sui generis*'. [21, p1035]. Elsewhere. Marx has also written 'with the production of relative surplus value, the entire real form of production is altered and a specifically capitalist mode of production comes into being (at the technology level too). Based on this, and simultaneously with it, the corresponding *relations of production* between the various agents of production and above all *between the capitalist and the wage labourer* comes into being *for the first time* [21, p1024, emphasis added].

PC equated capitalism with formal subsumption of labour, because according to him capital as relation is always present under formal subsumption [5, A86]. His position is not based on Marx as the above quotations indicate.

Dipankar Gupta [8] is more thorough in considering the Maxxian position regarding formal and real subsumption of labour. Unfortunately, he also has a mistaken notion that capital becomes the dominant force with the formal subsumption of labour. He bases his argument on the interpretation that the real subsumption revolutionises just the technology of production, the relation of production having already been revolutionised during the phase of formal subsumption. His position could be contradicted on the basis of Marx's *own* text as the above passages indicate.

The role of productive recycling of surplus in the context of the transition to capitalism should be adequately emphasised. The real subsumption, which can provide the foundations for the introduction of formal subsumption in new branches of industry helps capitalist production process to develop its sway over the society so that the domination of old precapitalist mode is over and the society becomes a capitalist society. The real subsumption appears as a result of the capitalist act of revolutionising the technology[8] which again is the outcome of productive recycling of surplus. To the capitalist production process it appears as the reproduction on an extended scale. Thus reproduction on an extended scale, or productive recycling of surplus developing real subsumption, works as a powerful lever for the development of the hegemony of capitalism. Be that a Prussian path or an America path, such a process of transformation was always visible in case of those countries where the transition was completed before the era of capitalist imperialism had set in. To repeat, it started with the process of development of a formal subsumption of labour which 'does not affect the mode of production' [21, p1010] but which created the basis for the development of real subsumption. The real subsumption which had appeared consequent to the productive recycling of capital then extended the area of formal subsumption and consequently the sway of capital, i.e., the domination of the capitalist mode of production set in. One point that is to be noted in this context is that the development from formal to real subsumption, however, is not automatic. There exist the necessity of a minimum amount of capital for the real subsumption of labour under capital to come about [21, p1027, p1035]. Such a necessary condition was, of course, satisfied by those countries where the transition was completed before the beginning of the era of imperialism, when capitalism had relentlessly pursued the policy of promoting technological progress.

In the era of imperialism, on the other hand, this transition might not be attained at all. Imperialism's economic foundation is monop-

---

8. The causal correspondence between real subsumption and revolutioning of technology can be expressed in the following way. The search for a constant increase in surplus value production implies a search for constant reduction in the necessary labour which is attained by constant expansion of technology when lengthening of working hours is not possible. Thus, the increase in relative surplus value is caused by the revolutionisation of technology.

oly which 'generally engenders a tendency to stagnation and decay' [10, p276]. 'Since monopoly prices are established even temporarily, the motive cause of technical and, consequently, of all other progress disappears to a certain extent, and further *economic* possibility arises of deliberately retarding technical progress' [10, p276]. The colonies and other dependent regions bear the major brunt of this technological retardation. The capitalist growth there, remains slow due to poor level of investment which is the result of imperialist policy of investing only the surplus capital in the dependent regions[9]. As a result, in the precapitalist sector, namely traditional agriculture, the forms of exploitation do not change. Even if the elements of formal subsumption are feebly present, there is hardly any real subsumption because there does not exist the minimum amount of capital that had to be recycled so that real subsumption could develop. Consequently, the domination of capitalist mode of production with respect to agriculture remains an impossibility.

As a typical example of such a situation, one may refer to a case described in an excellent study [7] on the process of depeasantisation in Bengal and Bihar during 1885-1947. This study establishes that there had been a phenomenal growth of land transfer following the enactment of Bengal Tenancy Act [1885] as a result of which there had been a large scale depeasantisation in Bengal and Bihar. But, this did not give rise to productive recycling of surplus to agriculture to a noticeable extent. The minimum amount of capital which is required for real subsumption of labour being thus non-available, agriculture did not betray the signs of the domination of capitalist mode of production.

It should be noted that the productive recycling of surplus in Agriculture is not arrested, under such a situation, due to the preponderance of conspicuous consumption, as had been the case under feudalism. Bengali *jotedars* who had benefited from Bengal Tenancy Act [1885] were not as consumption prone as were the Bengali zamindars. They even used to recycle their surplus for maximising their return, but such recycling did not give rise to technological innovation that could pave the way for real subsumption, because, as it happened at that time, usury-absolute-ground-rent combination had been higher than the expected rate of profit from

---

9. See Lenin [10], Chapter IV.

self-cultivation.[10] The theoretical possibility of the perpetuation of the usury-absolute-ground-rent combination until thc output raising innovation attains a certain critical minimum has also been pointed out elsewhere[11].

We are mentioning all these in order to arrive at a very important point. Semi-feudalism as a transitional stage implied that capitalism is its logical destiny, because, under such situations formal subsumption of labour would necessarily give rise to real subsumption by revolutionising the production techniques, the minimum capital for such real subsumption being always available. Our understanding is that in the era of imperialism, for the agriculture of the dependent countries such a development might be very slow because imperialism itself operates as a major deterrant to such transition to capitalism[12] As a result, semi-feudalism might appear as a transitional stage that perpetuates itself longer than what had been in Europe.

The logical possibility of the perpetual existence of such a pattern appears due to the perpetually poor level of recycling of surplus to agriculture such that the necessary minimum for the real subsumption of labour is hardly attained. The perpetually poor level of recycling of surplus to agriculture was also the *sine qua non* of feudal agriculture. What distinguishes a semi-feudal agriculture from a feudal agriculture is that, although in both cases agricultural surplus is siphoned off, in semi-feudal agriculture it is recycled for furthering the return, whereas in feudal agriculture it is consumed away. It should also be noted that under semi-feudalism, the owner of means

---

10. Utsa Patnaik pointed out the theoretical possibility of such a situation in her reply [25] to R. Sau 34]. That the Bengal jotedars had such a consideration, is evidenced by [36, p44-47], among many others.

11. See Bhaduri [3]. We are mentioning his equations (24) and (29).

12. The view that the presence of imperialism thwarts the transition to capitalism in colonies and semi-colonies is a classical view of the Marxists. Thus, Mao-Zedong points out 'imperialism is moribund capitalism'. But just because it is dying, it is all the more dependent on colonies and semi-colonies for survival and will certainly not allow any colony or semi-colony to establish *anything like a capitalist society* under the leadership of its own bourgeoisie' [18, p354-355, emphasis added]. Imperialism itself would not also promote a capitalist transition in the colonies and semi-colonies. Thus, it was resolved by the sixth congress of the Communist International (1929) that 'everywhere imperialism attempts to preserve and to perpetuate all those precapitalist forms of exploitation which serve as the basis for the existence of its reactionary allies (quoted here from [16] p312).

of production does not recycle the surplus to agriculture simply because, the returns from alternative investment channels is higher than the existing or expected rate of return from agriculture. These alternative investment channels pull in agricultural surplus so that investment in agriculture is discouraged. As a result, the process of real subsumption of labour is arrested and a backwardness perpetuates even in the relational dimension of capital.

II

Thus, we enter the core of the present problematic. On the basis of the primary data collected from a moderately advanced district of West Bengal, we attempt to study, the modes of surplus-use in the rural economy. The pivotal element of the study is, of course, the existence and extent of domination of the semi-feudal mode of surplus-use, which, as discussed earlier, has a crucial role in the perpetuation of agrarian backwardness.

In order to operationalise such a study, we start with the recognition of the fact that in every society there exist contradictions among various modes of production. One of these modes of production is dominant, the character of which determines the character of the society[13]. Following this methodology, when we hold the view that the Indian rural society is a semi-feudal society, we, in essence, describe the following situation. There are various modes of production in rural India. One of these modes of production is to be a dominant mode of production[14]. In Indian case, this dominant mode is the semi-feudal mode of production that combines foundation and capitalism.

The mapping of such a statement to the empirical world is never trivial. 'The translation of the 'algebra' of theory into the arithmetic of field notes or the statistics of censuses and vice versa are, at the

---

13. For example, 'in capitalist society, capitalism has changed its position from being a subordinate force in the old feudal era to being the dominant force, and the nature of society has accordingly changed from feudal to capitalist. In the new capitalist era, the feudal forces changed from their former dominant position to a subordinate one' [17, p333-334].

14. For 'semi-feudalism' as a transitional stage, the situation need not necessarily be so. It is one example of such a situation when '(the contradictions) seem to be in equilibrium which is however only *temporary* and relative' [17, p333, emphasis added].

best of times, the major difficulty of the social sciences - more so with a problematic loaded with conceptual ambivalence and a politically tense situation' [35, p84]. However, there exists rich literature on the subject because leaders and associated intellectuals of the communist parties all over the globe had to tackle this problem in order to draw a differentiation among peasants so that the enemies and the friends of the revolution could be distinguished. No serious Marxist could avoid this debate, because the question of drawing a line of distinction between friends and enemies 'is a question of prime importance for the revolution' [14, p18].

Following marxist classics, we developed the empirical correspondence of our problematic in the following way. Given various modes of production which describe a complex social reality, the first line of distinction among various modes could be drawn on the basis of the differences in the forms of exploitation. The associated modes of surplus use corresponding to various types of exploiters could be considered thereafter. From such a study, the hypothesis that there exists various modes of surplus use, corresponding to various modes of surplus generation, could be tested. In the course of such an exercise, the distinguishing features of the semi-feudal mode of surplus use and the extent of spread of such a mode could also be studied.

While drawing the first line of distinction among various modes on the basis of the differences in the forms of exploitation, the necessary theoretical clues could be derived from Lenin [12] and Mao [15] who formulated class analyses of the Russian and the Chinese societies respectively. With respect to surplus-earning landowners – identification of which is particularly necessary in the context of the mode of surplus use – Lenin distinguished between two classes, namely the big peasants [Grossbauern] and the big landowners. Both the classes, as a rule, employ hired labourers. However, while the first type takes part in manual labour in his farms the second does not. Exploitation through land rent is not mentioned except in case of the second group which used to lease out a part of its holdings to the tenant farmers. The form of exploitation in this case is mentioned as indirect exploitation of wage labour. The implication is that the tenants lease in land and pay the landlord a ground rent. The rent accrued by the landlord is a capitalist ground rent which is nothing but an indirect exploitation of wage labour[15]. There is, however, a striking dissimilarity between the position of

Mao and that of Lenin on the question of the treatment of ground rent. Lenin considers it as 'indirect exploitation of wage labour' and does not give it any special recognition. Only 'labour hiring' comes as the index for differentiating classes in the rural area. Mao-Zedong, on the other hand, included rent exploitation separately as an index for carrying out such differentiations.

It is not difficult to find the root of such a difference in approach. Lenin was considering the problem of differentiation in the context of such a country where capitalism had established its sway over agriculture so that the character of rent had changed substantially - it had become capitalist ground rent which was nothing but a part of surplus value [see footnote 15] and therefore it need not be included as a separate index. Mao, on the other hand, was considering a backward country where capitalism was yet to attain a dominant position. Given improper development of the land market, the phenomenon of differential ground rent that arises out of capitalist competition for control over better soil[16] is seldom present in such societies. The rent is, in the main, an absolute ground rent which arises from private ownership of land by a small section of feudal proprietors. The exploitation is not through wage labour, but through rack-renting. Associated with this, there is usury exploitation effected through an interlinkage between tenancy and credit. All such phenomena, which are distinctly different from the forms of exploitation under capitalism, are described by considering the phenomenon of exploitation of tenants by leasing out land.

In the context of the study of Indian Society, our understanding is that the Chinese case or the Maoist position is more relevant than the Russian case, because the outward symptoms of the prevalence of a precapitalist mode of production are very much present in India. We, therefore, start with the Maoist position regarding differentia-

---

15. Such a rent is a combination of both absolute and differential ground rents. The differential rent arises' from the surplus from the super profit, that is created by the more productive labour on better soil or on better located plot' Absolute ground rent, on the other hand, is possible only as a deduction from the available quantity of values for the benefit of the landowner, a deduction from the mass of surplus value - therefore, it implies either a deduction of profits or a deduction from wages' (Kautsky, as quoted by Lenin in [12, p299]).

16. See Lenin [12, p297].

tion among the peasants, particularly the surplus earning classes in the rural areas.

Mao-Zedung's method of differentiation has been described in his article 'How to Differentiate the Classes in the Rural Areas' [15]. Mao identifies there two broad types of exploiters [surplus-earners] in the rural areas; first, the landlord who 'does not engage in labour himself... and lives by exploiting the peasants. *The collection of land rent is his main form of exploitation*. In addition, he may lend money, hire labour or engage in industry and commerce. But his extraction of land rent from peasants is his principal form of exploitation' [ibid, p137, emphasis added]. The rich peasant, on the other hand, either owns or leases in land on which he engages his own labour and the labour of others. 'His main form of exploitation is hiring of labour [long term labourers]. In addition, he may let part of his land and practice exploitation through land rent or may lend money and engage in industry and commerce' [ibid, p137].

Apparently the rich peasant as a class is homogeneous and could be noted as 'Grossbauern', who is a vehicle of capitalist development in the rural areas. But a deeper probe reveals that in the context of a semi-feudal country like China, rich peasants were not necessarily considered a homogeneous class serving as vehicles of capitalism; a sizeable section of the rich peasantry was presumed to practice such exploitations which are of semi-feudal nature. Mao himself admits this when he comments,'most of the rich peasants in China are semi feudal in character' [16, p323]. This is not just a passing comment. Even during the final phase of the agrarian revolution, Mao was found to have distinguished between 'capitalist rich peasants' and 'rich peasants of semi-feudal nature'.[17]

In fact, the Chinese Communist Party while promulgating agrarian reform laws, issued instructions to the party workers to distinguish between a 'capitalist rich peasant' and 'rich peasant of semi-feudal nature'. In order to provide the worker with a guideline for carrying out such a distinction, a supplementary note with 'How to Analyse Classes' was issued. This defines a rich peasant of semi-landlord nature [elsewhere called semi-feudal rich peasant] as follows : 'If the area of land rented out by a rich peasant exceeds in size the land cultivated jointly by himself and by hired labourers, he shall

17. See for example 'Request for Opinion on the Tactics for dealing with Rich peasants' in [19] p24-25.

be referred to as a rich peasant, of a semi-landlord type'[18]. The supplementary note also states that a family with its members engaged in agriculture would be branded not as a rich peasant but as a landlord, if the area rented out 'is three times or more the size of land cultivated jointly by the family and the hired labourers'[19].

What do we cull from all these? Broadly speaking, there were two surplus-earning classes in China, viz., the landlord and the rich peasant. Whereas the landlords do not participate in production, the rich peasants do engage in labour themselves. But this is not the only line of distinction between the two. Even a rich peasant may be called a landlord or a semi-landlord if the area rented out be more than 3/4 or more than 1/2 but less than 3/4 of total holding of the family, respectively[20].

With respect to Indian agriculture, such a line of differentiation might not be very useful because of low incidence of tenancy in India. We, therefore, used a line of differentiation which is moderately different from the Chinese line. However, the basic approach remained the same. Thus with respect to the component of exploitation through ground rent we largely followed the Chinese method and considered two classes[21], namely, 'absentee' [in the sense of non-participation in the production process] and 'semi-absentee'. An 'absentee' is such an owner of the soil who leases out more than 3/4 of his own holding and does not lease in. His main source of income is the collection of ground rent[22]. On the other hand, a

---

18. Quoted here from [9, p739]

19. Ibid.

20. Utsa Patnaik, while summarising the Maoist position [27], evidently missed this Maoist line concerning further differentiation among rich peasants. Her line of differentiation in the direction of 'proto-bourgeoisie', (labour hiring greater than rent) and 'proto-feudal' (Labour hiring at most as high as rent) does not follow the Chinese line as we expounded in the text.

21. We deliberately avoided terms like 'feudal landlord' or 'semi-landlord type rich peasants', because, there is a considerable controversy on the connotations of the nomenclatures, in the context of the Indian debate on the mode of production (For example both Rudra [30] and Patnaik [27] use the term 'landlord' with completely different connotations).

22. A combination of differential and absolute ground rent. The two components, however, could not be distinguished because 'in practice, ground rent does not present itself to us divided in parts, it is impossible to say, which part is differential rent and which part is absolute rent' (Kautsky as quoted in [12, p298]).

'semi-absentee' owner is a person who leases out around 50 per cent of his holdings [a slight modification of the Chinese case of 'rich peasant of
semi-landlord type]. This much from the component of his exploitation through ground rent.[23] Using the component of exploitation through the employment of outside labour we found it inadvisable to use a catch-all term like hired labour' because of the existing hetorogeneity of 'outside labour' particularly in the context of Bengal agriculture[24]. In fact, labour-time cannot work as a workable common denominator[25], as suggested by some [27] because, it simplifies the existing reality by ignoring the existing heterogeneity in labour time. 'To avoid this, one must have a multiplicity of indexes or else, again composite indexes of several components' [36, p87].

At the time of working on the differentiation problem, we did not have the opportunity of going through the Namchinov's method[26] of constructing a composite index. Other existing methods of finding a common denominator being unsatisfactory[27], we had decided not to apply such techniques. As a crude but sensible alternative, we decided to rank such households for whom the rent component was not dominant, firstly, in terms of certain suitable indicators. Instead of carrying out useless refinements of the data, we then applied a 'thumb-rule' to get a rough, tentative distinction between what could be called the 'enterprising rich peasants; and the 'rich peasants of non-enterprising nature.

In terms of surplus use, the rich peasants of non-enterprising nature were expected to betray the same nature of surplus use as were the 'semi-absentee' ype households, both of them were expected to

---

23. For a rough approximation, the reduction of this component in terms of income or labour days is unnecessary.

24. For a detailed discussion on the heterogeneity of 'hired labour' see [2] and [31].

25. Utsa Patnaik tried to derive a ratio of exploitation E, by reducing two components, namely rent exploitation and exploitation through wage labour in terms of a workable common yardstick, namely 'labour-time'. Her method simplifies the existing reality by constructing an index in terms of a homogeneous labour. This is simplification, because it ignores various types of labour as identified in [2] and [31].

26. For an excellent exposition of Nemchinov's method, see [35].

27. For an elaboration of this point, see Chapter IV.

discourage recycling of surplus to agriculture because of relatively low profitability of agriculture. We, therefore, lumped these two classes in one group. The recycling of surplus is discouraged also by the 'absentee' households, but that is not expected to occur due to any profit motive. Enterprising rich peasants are expected to recycle surplus to agriculture at a rate which is higher than that of any other class.

Thus, the *apriori* classification of rural households was done in such a way that the obstacles to recycling of surplus to agriculture could be studied properly. In the context of such a study, emphasis was given on highlighting the distinguishing features of the semi-feudal mode of surplus use, which, according to our hypothesis, work as the major deterrent to the development of capitalist agriculture. The temporal behaviour of the surplus use pattern which denotes the direction of the use of surplus was captured in the study by considering the pattern of asset formation over time.

The data on the basis of which the following empirical exercise has been carried out refers to a sample of households belonging to a small district of West Bengal. One should not, therefore, draw a set of generalised conclusions on the basis of the findings of the enquiry. The study serves the limited objective of highlighting the role of surplus use in explaining the agrarian stagnation. In order to draw a set of general conclusions pertaining to the existing patterns of surplus use and their relevance to the study on the mode of production in Indian agriculture, an academic exercise with wider a datebase is, however, necessary.

REFERENCES

1. Banaji, J. India and the Colonial Mode of Production: Comment, *Economic and Political Weekly*, December, 1975.
2. Bardhan, P and Rudra, A. Types of labour Attachment in Bengal Agriculture, *Economic and Political Weekly*, August, 1980.
3. Bhaduri, A. A Study in Agrarian Backwardness under Semi-Feudalism. *The Economic Journal*, March, 1973.
4. Chattopadhyay, P. On the Question of the Mode of Production in Indian Agriculture : A Preliminary Note, *Economic and Political Weekly*, March, 1972.
5. ——— Mode of Production in Indian Agriculture : An Anti-Kritik, *Economic and Political Weekly*, December, 1972.
6. ——— Mode of Production in Indian Agriculture : An Afterword, *Economic and Political Weekly*, June, 1980.
7. Choudhuri, Binay Bhusan. The Process of Depeasantation in Bengal and

Bihar, 1885 - 1947, *Indian Historical Review*, New Delhi, Vol. 2.
8. Gupta, D. Formal and Real Subsumption of Labour under Capital: The Instance of Share Cropping, *Economic and Political Weekly*, September, 1980.
9. Hinton, W. *Fanshan*, Penguin, 1972.
10. Lenin, V.I. Imperialism, the Highest Stage of Capitalism, *Collected-Works*, Vol.22, Progress Publishers, Moscow, 1974.
11. ——— Economic content of Narodnism, *Collected Works*, Vol.1, Progress Publishers, Moscow, 1972.
12. ——— The Agrarian Programme of Social Democracy in the First Russian Revolution, 1905 - 1907. Collected Works, Vol. 13, Progress Publishers, Moscow, 1972.
13. ——— Preliminary Draft Theses on the Agrarian Question, *collected Works*, Vol.30, Progress Publishers, Moscow, 1974.
14. Mao-Zedong, Analysis of the classes in Chinese Society, *Selected Works*, Vol.1, Perking, 1977.
15. ——— How to differentiate the Classes in the Rural Areas, *Selected Works*, Vol.1, Peking, 1977.
16. ——— The Chinese Revolution and the Chinese Communist Party, *Selected Works*, Vol.2, Peking, 1977.
17. ——— On Contradiction, *Selected Works*, Vol.1, Peking, 1977.
18. ——— On New Democracy, *Selected Works*, Vol.2, Peking, 1977.
19 ——— Request for Opinion on the Tactics for Dealing with Rich Peasants, *Selected Works*, Voi.5, Peking, 1977.
20. Marx, K. Capital, Vol.1, Progress Publishers, Moscow (date not mentioned).
21. ——— Capital, Vol.1, Penguin, 1979.
22. ——— Capital Vol.2, Progress Publishers, Moscow, 1967.
23. ——— Capital Vol.3. Progress Publishers,Moscow, 1968.
24. ——— Grundrisse, Penguin, 1973.
25. Patnaik, U. Empirical Identification of Peasant Classes Revisted, *Economic and Political Weekly*, March, 1980.
26. ——— On the Mode of Production in Indian Agriculture - A Reply, *Economic and Political Weekly*, September, 1972.
27. ——— Class Differentiation within the Peasantry, *Economic and Political Weekly*, September, 1976.
28. ——— Capitalist Development in Agriculture, *Economic and Political Weekly*, June, 1970.
29. Rudra, A. In search of the Capitalist Farmers, *Economic and Political Weekly*, June, 1970.
30. ——— Class Relation in Indian Agriculture - I, II & III, *Economic and Political Weekly*, June,1978.
31. ——— The Self Contained Village Society, Frontier, January, 1981.
32. Rudra, A., Majid, A. and Talib, B.D. - Big Farmers of Punjab: Some Preliminary Findings of a Sample Survey, *Economic and Political Weekly*, September, 1969.
33. Sau, R. On the Essence of Manifestation of Capitalism in Indian Agriculture, *Economic and Political Weekly*, September, 1979.
34. ——— A Theory of Rent and Agrarian Relation, *Economic and Political Weekly*, June, 1979.
35. Shanin, T. Measuring Peasant Capitalism, *Peasants in History* edited by E.J. Hobsbawm and others, Oxford University Press, 1980.
36. West Bengal Government. Report of the Land Revenue Commission, 1940, Vol. VI.

ONE

THE DISTRICT

GENERAL

A small but populous district, Nadia belongs to the eastern plains of West Bengal with a total geographical area of about 3926 sq km which is approximately 4.46 per cent of the total geographical area of the state. According to the 1971 census, the population density of the district is 568 persons per sq km as against 504 for West Bengal as a whole. In other words, Nadia supports about 5 per cent of the population of West Bengal with an approximately 4.56 per cent of its geographical area - a situation that brings out the district's relative overpopulation in sharp relief. The present position in this respect is, needless to say, still worse.

The high density of the population in the district can largely be attributed to a rather steady seepage of refugees into the district across the international border from Bangladesh or erstwhile East Pakistan since 1947. Two phenomenal migrations, one during the partition in 1947 and the other during the Bangladesh war, coupled with a steady growth of indigenous population have led to a three-fold rise in the district population over the last thirty years. With net cultivable area remaining nearly the same over this period, the man-land ratio in the district has considerably increased.

Influx of the refugees has only reinforced the occupational structure of the population of the district, because the refugees are mainly enterprising peasants, *Namasudra* by caste from Faridpur district of Bangladesh. Thus 81.26 per cent of the population of the district is living in the rural areas and cultivators together with agricultural labourers account for 65.30 per cent of the work force in the district.

It has been observed that the influx of refugees following the partition of Bengal also brought about a high rate of urban growth and a fast urbanisation in Nadia during the first decade following independence. During the next two decades, the pace of urban growth remained moderately high, but this was not coupled with even a nominal rise in urbanisation. Such a phenomenon could be explained in terms of the dwarfed growth of urban economic activities. A poor growth of industrial employment and a relative decline of 'services sector', the largest employment generating sector of urban Nadia in terms of work-force absorbtion, arrested the effectiveness of the 'urban pull' factor of the population movement. As a result, the migration from rural areas is largely discouraged and consequently, the pace of urbanisation in the district remains poor.[1]

Soil Condition

The soil of the district has largely originated from the deposition of silt carried by the river Ganga. And as expected, the soil structure varies from sandy loam to clay. In fact, except for the tract known as *Kalantar* and some portion of Ranaghat, the soil is light sandy loam, accounting for 78 per cent of the total cultivated area. This type of soil is in general deficient in organic matter and available nitrogen content is very low. That makes Nadia a relatively less fertile district. Again, as a result of the predominance of high land in the district, one observes a greater acreage of *aus* paddy in contrast to the general dominance of *aman* in West Bengal. Since the soil does not retain the water necessary for the cultivation of winter rice, the latter is not much observed. With the gradual decay of the river system, the soil is no longer benefitted from river silts. And although land is nowhere sterile, it is not generally very fertile either.

Rainfall and Irrigation

Although there is a network of rivers and streams, except for rainy seasons, these rivers and streams are mostly dry[2] and hence hardly

---

1. For a detailed discussion see [2]

2. For a brief discussion on the decay of Nadia's river system, see [3].

provide the district with the facilities of river lift irrigation, there are only 272 river lift irrigation pumps in the district. The other mode of surface irrigation, namely the canal irrigation is absolutely absent in the district. However, the district has an abundant resource of underground water. There exists a static water table, about 500 ft below the surface, that could be exploited with centrifugal pumps. As a result, Nadia has witnessed a phenomenal growth in the number of shallow and deep tubewells in recent years. By the end of the last decade, there were 517 deep tubewells and about 16000 shallow tubewell points in the district. This did not, however, change the absolute dependence of its agriculture on rainfall because only about 9.82 per cent of the gross cropped area of the district is irrigated by these tubewells.

Nadia, being near the tropic of cancer, experiences early monsoon. On an average, more than 50 per cent of the total precipitation is received during the months from May to July. Such a precipitation pattern suits jute and early autumn rice (*aus*) cultivation. The importance of *aus* and jute in the crop schedule of the district is thus only too natural. Apart from relatively early monsoon, Nadia's temperature makes the district suitable for sugarcane cultivation. The district is thus endowed with natural conditions that help adopting a diversified crop-mix, distinct from the common *aman* based monocrop cultivation prevalent in most part of West Bengal.

Land-holding pattern

The agrarian sector of the district is largely dominated by small and middle peasants. In fact, the number of large holdings as well as the area accounted for has steadily declined over the years. 1970 census data (Census of Agriculture) reveal that 77.82 per cent of the holdings in the district are below 5 acres and these together represent 43.75 per cent of the area under cultivation. On the other hand, only about 6 per cent of the holdings have land over 10 acres, constituting about 23 per cent of the cultivated areas. As indicated in table 1.1, the corresponding figures for the state exhibit similar features. Thus in terms of land holding pattern, Nadia can be treated as a representative district of West Bengal.

The number of holdings above 25 acres is virtually non-existent. So far as the 1951 census is concerned, 1.56 per cent of the holdings were listed under this category. Such holdings accounted for 13.41

per cent of the cultivated area. The corresponding figures for the state were 1.59 per cent and about 14 per cent respectively. Since the passing of the Estate Acquisition Act in 1953, this category is gradually dwindling to insignificance. Thus, 1970 Agricultural Census reports that only 0.82 per cent of the area under cultivation are controlled by such households (Table 1.1). The absence of very big holdings, at least officially, is in general confirmed also by the Land Records Department which noted that there were only 312 'Big Raiyots'[3] in the district in 1979. Our choice of big landowners should be received in this perspective.

Table 1.1 : Percentage Distribution of Number of Holdings (N) and Area under the Size Class (A) by Size Class

Size-Class (Acres)	WEST BENGAL 1951		WEST BENGAL 1970		NADIA 1951		NADIA 1970	
	N	A	N	A	N	A	N	A
0 - 5	70.67	32.32	82.30	47.25	63.32	29.96	77.82	43.75
5.01 - 10.00	21.21	30.10	13.23	28.93	24.92	31.68	16.51	33.20
10.01 - 25.00	6.63	23.29	4.38	19.24	10.19	25.41	5.60	22.13
25.01 and above	1.59	14.28	0.09	4.56	1.56	13.41	0.07	0.82

Source: -Census, 1951, from [3]
— World Agricultural Census, 1970, West Bengal, Board of Revenue, Directorate of Agriculture, Socio-Economic Evaluation Branch, Government of West Bengal, 1975.

The Place of Nadia in the Agrarian Economy of West Bengal

It is a common knowledge by now that since the mid-60s, West Bengal alongwith India witnessed a countrywide campaign for increasing production on the food front. The campaign was accompanied by the promotion of the HYV seeds and fertilisers. True, till recently some districts made definite headway in terms of adoption of new technology and there are signs that production conditions have also been modified in some districts. However, the progress over all is uneven. Broadly, the new strategy presumed, (i) a controlled irrigation system (ii) larger holding sizes with least fragmentations and (iii) a healthy tenurial arrangements, apart from (iv) many administrative

---

3. For definition, see chapter 2.

requirements conducive to the adoption of the new strategy. In general, most of the districts in West Bengal do not satisfy the stipulated requirements. Hence, compared to some states in Northern India, performance of West Bengal is lacklustre. Barring the districts like Burdwan, Birbhum, Hooghly and Murshidabad the spread of the new agricultural strategy in the state is not encouraging.

Table 1.2 : Performances of the Districts in Terms of Some Selected Economic Indicators

Districts	Cropping intensity 1979-80	Non-traditional Irrigation as percentage of gross cropped 1976-77	Index of Agricultural Production in 1979 - 80 (1970-71 = 100)	HYV Crop as percentage of gross cropped Area (1974-75)
Burdwan	1.33(9)	47.82(1)	147.80(2)	18.16(3)
Birbhum	1.34(7)	39.44(2)	108.89(9)	15.24(5)
Bankura	1.15(14)	27.06(4)	106.45(11)	7.37(10)
Midnapore	1.19(12)	13.36(5)	108.32(10)	9.22(8)
Howrah	1.34(8)	7.08(8)	91.87(15)	9.95(7)
Hooghly	1.58(4)	33.96(3)	132.81(3)	24.17(1)
24 Parganas	1.21(10)	2.83(11)	150.74(1)	5.61(11)
Nadia	1.69(2)	9.82(7)	125.49(5)	13.04(6)
Murshidabad	1.73(1)	11.25(6)	110.99(8)	18.31(2)
West Dinajpur	1.41(5)	2.18(13)	101.38(14)	8.43(9)
Malda	1.68(3)	3.23(10)	116.47(6)	15.46(4)
Jalpaiguri	1.21(11)	3.49(9)	116.16(7)	2.31(15)
Darjeeling	1.15(15)	2.37(12)	127.61(4)	2.77(14)
Cooch Behar	1.38(6)	1.22(14)	106.34(13)	3.06(12)
Purulia	1.16(13)	1.05(15)	106.41(12)	2.83(13)
West Bengal	1.35	13.75	119.41	8.32

Note : H Y V crop implies boro and wheat; figures in paranthesis denote rank positions.

Source : Economic Review, 1980-81
Data collected from the principal agricultural officer, various districts.

Nadia, however, can boast of moderate progress inspite of initial handicaps in the form of non-availability of irrigational facilities and backdated tenurial arrangements. But then, as pointed out above, there was a massive drive towards installation of deep and shallow tubewells which succeeded in pulling up Nadia in the state irrigation map. In spite of the absence of canal irrigation Nadia ranks 7th in terms of the percentage of non-traditional irrigation to gross cropped area (Table 1.2). The spread of irrigation has definitely helped Nadia to pull out of its mid-60s stagnation. There had been substantial increase in acreage for 'boro' production which had increased from meagre 2,200 hectares in 1964-65 to an average of 10500 hectares by mid-70s. There has been an increase in the acreage of wheat also, the production of which was virtually absent in the mid-60s. These crops together with sugarcane helped Nadia to practice fairly intensive cultivation and today Nadia ranks a close 2nd only behind Murshidabad in cropping intensity.

In terms of the growth of production of foodgrains, Nadia's performance is commendable. A point to point comparison of the index number of the production of foodgrains indicates that during the last decade, there was a 25.49 per cent increase in Nadia. The rate of growth was higher than the rate for the state as a whole. However, as the table 1.2 indicates, the performance of Nadia is not as spectacular as that of 24-Parganas or Burdwan where the growth rates were around 50 per cent. From the ranking of the districts, one gathers that the performance of Nadia in terms of growth of production of foodgrains is moderate.

Table 1.2 indicates that 13.04 per cent of the gross cropped area of the district is under the H Y V crops, viz., 'boro' - a summer paddy, and wheat. Compared to the achievements of Hooghly, Murshidabad and Burdwan, this is never spectacular. But, given the predominance of high land and not so wellspread irrigation facilities, Nadia's achievement is not insignificant - it speaks volume about the enterprise of its peasants. However, the rank position being 6, we conclude that the new agricultural strategy has made moderate progress in the district.

Considering all the four indicators, we find that in terms of all the indicators excepting the cropping intensity, Nadia is a middle-ranking district. It is neither an advanced district like Burdwan, nor a backward one like Purulia. Being a moderately advanced district, Nadia is therefore a region where the backward production conditions are expected to coexist with the advanced ones. Since a mode of surplus use correspond largely to the prevailing conditions of production, the position of Nadia vis-a-vis the production conditions makes it an ideal field area for the study of the features of both advanced and backward modes of surplus use and their interactions. Our choice of Nadia as the field area should be received in this perspective.

REFERENCES

1. Government of West Bengal: *Economic Review 1980-81* Statistical Appendix (1981).
——— : Directorate of Agriculture, *World Agricultural Census, West Bengal, 1970.* (1975)
——— : *District Statistical Handbook*, Various years.
2. Khasnabis, R. and Nath, N. *Urban Growth Without Urbanisation; The Experience of a Border District of West Bengal.* Paper presented to the Conference on Urban Development, Calcutta University, 1981 (Included in this volume).
3. Mitra, A. *An Account of Land Management in West Bengal, 1850-1950*, Census publication 1951.

TWO

SELECTION OF HOUSEHOLDS

The population

It had been decided that the study of the mode of surplus utilisation in West Bengal Agriculture with Nadia District as the field area would have big landowners as the point of reference. The rationale for such a choice was that the big landowners were expected to matter most on the question of the generation and utilisation of rural surplus because land had been the most important source of the latter[1]. The sample of rural households should, therefore, be drawn from a population of a size-class of landowners that could be termed 'big'. Thus the first problem was to identify such a population of big landowners.

A complete enumeration of the rural households with respect to the size of own holding being absent[2], the standard practice, while conducting such surveys, is to select some villages randomly and conduct the relevant enquiry with respect to some selected big landowners of those villages only. However, we did not have to follow

---

1. According to the All India Rural Debt and Investment Survey, (1971-72), 60.49 per cent of the rural assets in the eastern plains of West Bengal (the region where Nadia is situated) was in the form of agricultural land (see 2,20.2.3).

2. No official organisation including the Agricultural Census; 1970, had enumerated the rural households with respect to the size of own holdings. In recent years the *Panchayat Samitis* are stated to have prepared such records. However, most often these are perfunctory in nature. In Nadia, we did not get such records from the *Panchayat* offices.

this roundabout way because some *a priori* information about the big landowners of the district was available.

As will be recalled, the Land Records Department of the Government of West Bengal maintains the list of such households of the district which held agricultural lands above the level of ceilings[3] imposed by the Land Reforms Act, 1971(LR,1971). This list could serve as the primary basis for locating the population of big landowners because the ceiling is imposed on the holdings of the big landowners only.

The Big Raiyots

The list of such landowners is prepared by the Settlement Circle Office in the following way. The LR, 1971 made it obligatory for such raiyots whose lands were expected to come under the provision of the ceiling, to submit a declaration to the settlement officer (according to clause 7 A of LR, 1971) concerning the level of holdings in the possession of the raiyots. On the basis of these declarations and also on the basis of some *suo moto* cases, the settlement office is instructed to prepare a list of households that would come under the purview of the new ceiling applied to ownership holdings. This comprises the Big Raiyot register of the district. By consulting this register, one might prepare a list of big landowners of the district.

In 1978, the total number of cases appearing in the Big Raiyot registrar of Nadia were 1850. Out of these, 1035 were in the Krishnanager subdivision, the rest belonged to the Ranaghat subdivision. However, only 312 of these cases were legally liable to the application of the ceiling. The block-wise break up of these cases is given in table 2.1, column 1. It indicates that the largest number of Big Raiyot cases appeared in Hanskhali, the lowest number was in

---

3. Section 14M of West Bengal Land Reforms Act defines the ceiling area as follows:

i) 2.5 hectaes of irrigated land or 3.5 hectares of unirrigated lands for a family consisting of one person (adult unmarried or sole surviving member of a family).

ii) For a family consisting of not more than 5 members 5.0 hectares of irrigated land or 7 hectares of unirrigated lands.

iii) For a family of more than 5 members, an additional 0.5 hectare of irrigated or 0.7 hectare of unirrigated land for each additional member subject to a maximum of 7 hectares of irrigated or 9.8 hectares (24.3 acres) of unirrigated agricultural land (Ref. 6, p.16).

Haringhata.

Table 2.1 : Blockwise distribution of the big landowners and the Villages covering the big landowners

Block	Big Landowners: Cases from Big Raiyot Register	Big Landowners: Cases from local sources	Villages in the block	Villages covering the population[a]
	(1)	(2)	(3)	(4)
Haringhata	6	2	90	6
Chakda	15	8	139	20
Ranaghat I	17	13	81	23
Hanskhali	49	22	72	32
Santipur	19	15	84	24
Ranaghat II	51	10	107	36
Kaliganj	6	9	127	15
Nakasipara	26	11	109	30
Krishna nagar I	12	11	59	22
Krishna nagar II	5	10	78	15
Tehatta I	14	14	40	25
Tehatta II	17	13	56	27
Karimpur	26	5	151	23
Charpra	26	5	84	23
Nabadwip	8	5	28	13
Krishnaganj	15	13	55	24
Total	312	166	1360	358

Notes (a) Cases from Big Raiyot Register as well as cases from level sources.
(b) Sources: Big Raiyot cases were collected from the Big Raiyot Register' of Land Settlement Offices. Information on the number of villages in the block was collected from Census 1971 and the relevant offices of the panchayat samities.

The Alternative Source

There are, however, problems with the Big Raiyot register. There are households, in the rural areas who evaded the Ceiling by taking recourse to clandestine sale or gift in good time. Some households have kept the holding legally below the ceiling by giving away the surplus land to non-existent persons (*benami*). There are various other methods of retaining land above the ceiling level. These evasive raiyots in the rural areas could not have been traced, had we moved only on the basis of the Big Raiyot Register of the Land

Records Office.

In order to overcome this difficulty, it has subsequently been decided that the Big Raiyot register would not be the only basis of locating the population. Although a high percentage of the surveyed households (about 75 per cent) had been selected randomly from the list of the Big Raiyots, a significant proportion was selected from some other sources. While surveying households in a block, selected on the basis of the Big Raiyot Register, the name of such substantial households who, for some reason or other, did not come under the purview of the ceiling law were also collected. The source of this information was people with deep rural roots, viz., local panchayat leaders, tahasildars and local leaders of important kishan organisations who keep information about big landowners. On the basis of this information, another sample was drawn so that the limitations of the Big Raiyot Register could be overcome.

166 households, explaining about 34 per cent of the population were traced in this way. The blockwise distribution of such households is given in column 2 of table 1.2.

The Villages Covering the Population

According to the 1971 census, there were 1360 villages in Nadia. 478 households that constituted the population were spread over only 358 villages. The population spread over about 28.5 per cent of total villages of the district (table 2.1), also indicates that majority of the villages were from Krishnanagar subdivision. With respect to the coverage of villages by the population of big landowners, the inter block variation is extremely high. There exist, at one extreme, blocks like Tehatta I where the population of big landowners covered as much as 62.5 per cent of the villages. On the other extreme, there are blocks like Haringhata where only about 6.6 per cent of total villages were covered by the population.

The Sample Design

We selected 152 households out of a population of 478 big landowners. 100 out of these 152 households were selected randomly from 312 'Big Raiyot'. The rest came from a purposive selection from 166 big landowners, the primary information about whom was gathered from non-official local sources.

The random selection of 100 cases from the Big Raiyot Register of the Land Records Department was performed after stratifying the population. The major stratification variable was the quantitative performance of each block in terms of certain economic indicators.

The Zones as Strata

There exists a considerable heterogeneity among blocks with regard to performances in terms of agricultural activities. This is revealed through high values of standard deviations and coefficients of variation of some indicators selected for recording the economic performance of each block (table 2.2). The heterogeneity of block is expected to have some impact on the methods of surplus generation and its utilisation practiced by the selected households. For example, the big farms in the economically advanced zones are expected to be endowed more with the facilities of advanced production conditions which, in its turn, help develop capitalist mode of surplus generation and its utilisation at a higher proportion than what might have been found in other zones. In order to tackle this problem, it was proposed to bunch the blocks according to homogeneous economic zones. A random sampling with zones as strata with sample fractions selected on the basis of suitable weight for each zone was then performed.

The Selection of Weights : Cluster Analysis

In order to differentiate the zones in terms of economic advancement, we selected four economic indicators and recorded the performance of each block in terms of each of the indicators. Agriculture being the most important activity of the zones, the indicators were so chosen as to measure the existing level of performance of agricultural operation and the propensity to accept the new agricultural strategy. The relevant indicators are (1) Intensity of cultivation (2) Yield (of principal crops) per acre (3) Extent of non-traditional irrigation and (4) Area under the H Y V crops.

Data being available (Table 2.2) on these four indicators over sixteen relevant blocks, we were faced with the problem of reducing the scores of each block in terms of alternative indicators into a common one so that the performance of blocks could be compared and bunching of blocks in the form of advanced, moderate and backward zones could be done.

Table 2.2 : Quantitative performance of various blocks in terms of certain selected Indicators.

	Intensity of cultivation[1]	Yield per acre[2] (kg)	Non-traditional irrigation as p.c. of total irrigated area (1976-77).	Area under H.Y.V.[3] as p.c. of cropped gross area.
Haringhata	172.19	481.32	53.43	56.05
Chakdah	147.4	496.67	26.45	32.27
Rahaghat I	157.69	368.85	33.37	32.22
Hanskhali	150.81	369.24	26.74	42.68
Santipur	167.51	424.70	29.06	11.98
Ranaghat II	130.93	405.75	27.02	24.87
Kaliganj	163.56	394.39	26.92	16.36
Nakasipara	146.80	387.17	26.15	21.23
Krishnanagar II	161.60	331.47	22.58	24.74
Krishnanagar I	137.60	356.90	26.84	20.38
Tehtta I	144.10	393.60	25.90	8.73
Tehatta II	143.80	388.40	15.11	7.36
Karimpur	179.09	345.39	15.73	13.97
Chapra	152.00	379.96	20.31	6.25
Nabadwip	171.40	343.51	16.62	12.19
Krishnaganj	137.23	365.42	13.28	10.14
S.D.	13.71	44.35	9.12	13.42
C.V.	0.09	0.11	0.36	0.63

Note: 1. $\frac{\text{Gross cropped area}}{\text{Net cropped area}} \times 100$ during 1976-77

2. Average of aman and aus paddy, during 1972-73 and 1976-77.

3. Boro and wheat during 1976-77.

Source: A resume of Agricultural Development in Nadia 1976-'77, Principal Agricultural Officer, Nadia, Krishnanagar.

Kendall's method[4] of forming clusters was the statistical device used by us for bunching the blocks in terms of advanced, moderate and backward zones. This method suggest that we construct the correlation matrix with the values of each of the four variables mentioned above. The weights are then so chosen that the inner product of the vector of weights equals the maximum eigen value of the correlation matrix. The maximum eigen value is 2.307 and the weights are 0.281,0.723, 0.939, 0.896. These weights are now used to derive

---

4. For a detailed discussion, see [4].

the linear combinations and the clusters emerge from them. The final results are set forth in table 2.3.

A suggested alternative was the principal component analysis. Reducing the data to standard normal deviates as suggested by Johnston[5], we applied this method which distributes the 'between block variation' 'among the indicators, disturbing 'within block variation' as little as possible. This enables us to bunch the block among different zones. Technical details of the method could be found in Anderson[6]. The maximum eigen value was 0.4317718; corresponding eigen vertor is (0.5346505, 0.5923781, -0.2034992, 0.7431672). These elements were used as weights to find out the linear combination. The blocks were then conveniently drawn out into 3 groups (Table 2.3).

Results obtained from these two alternative methods differ marginally. Two elements in moderate zone obtained from Kendall's cluster analysis move down to backward zone when the alternative analysis is applied. Two other elements, however move up to moderate from backward zones. Other elements do not change their positions.

Table 2.3 : Classification of Zones According to Three Alternative Methods

A. Zones classified according to Cluster Analysis (Kendall)		
Advanced	**Moderate**	**Backward**
1. Haringhata	1. Ranaghat II	1. Karimpur
2. Chakdah	2. Kaliganj	2. Tehatta-I
3. Ranaghat-I	3. Nakasipara	3. Tehatta-II
4. Hanskhali	4. Krishnanagar II	4. Chapra
5. Santipur	5. Krishnanagar I	5. Nabadwip
		6. Krishnaganj
B. Zones classified according to Principal Component Analysis		
Advanced	**Moderate**	**Backward**
1. Haringhata	1. Kaliganj	1. Krishnaganj
2. Chakdah	2. Karimpur	2. Tehatta-I
3. Santipur	3. Krishnanagar II	3. Tehatta-II
4. Ranaghat-I	4. Nabadwip	4. Krishnanagar-I
5. Hanskhali	5. Nakasipara	5. Chapra
		6. Ranaghat-II

5. See [3, p.326].

6. See [1, chapter 11]

C. **Zones classified according to 'Thumb Rule'**

Advance	**Moderate**	**Backward**
1. Santipur	1. Hanskhali	1. Krishnanagar I
2. Ranaghat I	2. Ranaghat II	2. Krishnanagar II
3. Chakdah	3. Kaliganj	3. Nabadwip
4. Haringhata	4. Karimpur	4. Chapra
		5. Krishnaganj
		6. Tehatta -I
		7. Tehatta -II
		8. Nakaspara

Note : Prepared on the basis of table 2.2; see text for explation.

The absence of major variation in results is explained by the fact that the weights do not differ significantly when drawn by alternative methods.

Being convinced that there is no need to switch over to principal component analysis because the results hardly differ, we tried to consider how far the results were sensible from economic point of view. Mainly depending on economic logic, we developed a method of finding a suitable index by ranking the blocks in terms of performance with respect to each indicator as above or below the district average. When a block is found to score below the district average in terms of an indicator, we rank it Backward (B) with respect to that indicator. Similarly, a block is ranked Advanced (A) with respect to a particular indicator, if the score is above district average. Thus, every block has four such rank marks. Homogeneity in terms of rank marks,i.e., the existence of all A or all B for a particular block makes the bunching problem simple. Zones with all A scores are decidedly advanced. Similarly, zones with all B scores are backward zones. Heterogeneity in rank marks create a difficult problem. We considered each such case separately and tried to understand economic implication of each combination and applying a rule of thumb, we solved the problem of classification in such cases. The results are given in table 2.4.

Such a 'Thumbrule' approach which is sensible from the economic point of view gives the results which differ marginally from those obtained from other two approaches. This enables us to conclude that the results obtained from first two methods generally and those from Kendall's method particularly are economically sensible and bunching of zones in terms of that index is meaningful from the economic point of view.

Table 2.4 : Division of Nadia District into Economically Advanced, Moderate and Backward Zones (Thumb Rule)

	Criteria				
	Intensity of cultivation	Yield/ acre	Area under H Y V	Non-traditional irrigation	Classification
1. Krishnanagar I	B	B	B	A	Backward
2. Krishnanagar II	A	B	B	B	Backward
3. Nabadwip	A	B	B	B	Backward
4. Chapra	B	B	B	B	Backward
5. Krishnaganj	B	B	B	B	Backward
6. Tehatta I	B	B	B	B	Backward
7. Tehatta II	B	B	A	B	Backward
8. Nakasipara	B	B	B	A	Backward
9. Karimpur	A	B	A	B	Moderate
10. Kalaiganj	A	B	B	A	Moderate
11. Santipur	A	A	B	A	Advanced
12. Hanskhali	B	B	A	A	Moderate
13. Ranaghat I	B	A	A	A	Advanced
14. Ranaghat II	B	B	A	A	Moderate
15. Chakdah	B	A	A	A	Advanced
16. Haringhata	A	A	A	A	Advanced

Source : Table 2.2

One interesting observation is that the classification scheme conforms to three well-defined geographical regions of the district. The advanced zone conforms broadly to the southern region, the moderate to the middle region and the backward to the northern region. We consider such clustering in geographical region as a supporting evidence of a well defined zonal classification of blocks.

The Drawing of Samples

The zones represent the strata on which the samples were to be drawn. The values of the indicators alongwith the number of households occurring in each zone were used to derive the sample proportions.

The values of an indicator were aggregated over the three zones and the result was reduced to a proportion of 100. Once we had this for all the indicators zonewise, we aggregated them er zones, and again reduced them to percentages. Now we consider the percentage number of households occurring in each zone; multiplying the proportion arrived from indicators in each zone by the population proportion of the same zone, and again reducing them to proportion of 100, we arrived at the final proportion. Since the actual number of samples we intended to draw is 100, the above proportions give the number of samples to be drawn from each zone. The numbers are: 42 cases from the advanced zone, 32 from moderate and 26 from the backward zones.

Some of the blocks have relatively less representation in the population of households. We did not want to miss them. We, therefore, preferred a drawing where it is equally spaced out over the population, and the gaps are relatively less. Hence our preference for circular systematic sampling to other existing methods. In this method, the ratio of population to sample value is taken as the gap between two successive units of the sample. In cases it is a fraction, this gap is rounded off. Now considering the population to be lying along a circle, the samples can be drawn over it on the specified gap. The starting point can be chosen from the random number table. The technicalities of the method can be found in Murthy [5].

The population having been listed, the samples were drawn. The number of households drawn by stratified random sample from each block can be had from table 2.5.

The Purposive Selection

Another 52 households were selected from the list of 166 big landowners prepared on the basis of local information. This selection was purposive. While visiting a block, a list of some (roughly about 50 per cent of 'Big Raiyot' cases in the block) substantial households not appearing in the Big Raiyot Register was prepared. Out of these households, a purposive selection, covering about 50 percent of randomly selected households, was made. The basis of the selection was the existence of prima facie evidence in favour of the hypothesis that the relevant household had been incurring productive recycling of surplus either in agriculture or in rural tertiary activities in a significant way. The blockwise and zonewise distribution of such selected households is given in table 2.5.

Needless to say, the element of purposiveness introduced in the sample, inhibit statistically valid generalisation with respect to the big landowners of the district.

The Households Visited

Out of 152 selected households, we could collect relevant information about 138 households (table 2.5). Thus, about 10 per cent of the total cases had to be dropped. Insufficient information, particularly on asset formation, was the reason for dropping 6 such cases. The respondents were hostile in 4 cases. Another 4 cases, collected from the Big Raiyot register seemed non-substantive with regard to asset position.[7] We found it necessary to drop these 4 cases also.

Among 138 households, there were two households belonging to two zones bordering the district boundary. It was so reported that a substantive part of their lands had been in the adjacent districts. Amount of such lands could not be ascertained since we followed an indirect method[8] according to which it was necessary to visit the settlement offices of Burdwan and 24 parganas, a task that could not be carried out due to the paucity of time and fund. However, on the basis of the supplementary evidences,it was concluded that these households had been 'absentee'[9]. Other relevant information being also available, it was decided not to drop these two cases altogether. We preserved them in the sample except while analysing the information on land. The sample of the subsequent analysis is, therefore, 138, except in case of the analysis of the information on owned land of the respondents, when the sample base is reduced to 136. Since the aforesaid households belong to the group of 'absentee', the number of respondents in the absentee group is reduced to 25 while analysing the information on owned land of the absentee households.

---

7. These were *suo moto* cases. Probably the settlement office wrongly identified them as 'Big Raiyots'.

8. See section on Estimation of Owned Land, Chapter 3.

9. For explanation of the term, see section on, Surplus Earning Classes in Nadia, Chapter 4.

Table 2.5 : Blockwise/Zonewise Distribution of Sample Households

Zones/Blocks	Stratified Random Sample		Purposive Selcetion	
	Selected	Visited	Selected	Visited
Advanced				
Haringhata (AH)	2	2	1	1
Chakdah (AC)	5	4	2	2
Ranaghat I (AR)	6	5	3	3
Hanskhali (AHK)	21	19	5	4
Santipur (AS)	8	5	7	7
Total Advanced Zone	42	35	18	17
Moderate				
Ranaghat II (MR)	17	14	5	4
Kaliganj I (MK)	2	2	1	1
Nakasipara (MN)	9	9	5	5
Krishnanagar I (MK_1)	3	3	2	2
Krishnanagar II (MK_2)	1	1	1	1
Totai Moderate Zone	32	29	14	13
Backward				
Tehatta I (BT1)	3	3	2	2
Tehatta II (BT2)	5	5	6	6
Karimpur (BK)	6	6	3	3
Chapra (BC)	6	6	5	5
Nabadwip (BN)	2	2	2	2
Krishnaganj (BKJ)	4	3	2	1
Total Backward Zone	26	25	20	19
Total	100	89	52	49

Source: As in Table 2.1

The villagewise distribution of sample households had also been given in table 2.6. It shows that one village - one household correspondence was maintained in case of 9 blocks. The correspondence was disturbed mainly in case of Hanskhali, Ranaghat II and Tehatta II Blocks, where 23, 18 and 11 households were included from 15, 14 and 7 villages respectively. In aggregate, 138 households included in the study were selected from 118 villages of the district.

Table 2.6: Village-wise Distribution of Sample Households

Block	Households visited	Villages covering the household
Haringhata (AH)	3	2
Chakdah (AC)	6	6
Hanskhali (AHK)	23	15
Santipur (AS)	12	12
Ranaghat I (AR)	8	8
Ranaghat II (MR)	18	14
Kaliganj I (MK_I)	3	3
Nakasipara (MN)	14	14
Krishnanagar I (MK_I)	5	5
Krishnanagar II (MK_{II})	2	2
Tehatta I (BT_I)	5	4
Tehatta II (BT_{II})	11	7
Karimpur (BK)	9	8
Chapra (BC)	11	10
Nabadwip (BN)	4	4
Krishnaganj (BKJ)	4	4
Total	138	118

Note: Excluding Kalyani P.S. and Municipal areas of the District.
Source: Table 2.5 and District Census Handbook (1971).

REFERENCE

1. Anderson, T.W. *An Introduction to Multivariate Statistical Analysis,* Wiley Eastern Private Limited, New Delhi, 1972.
2. Govt. of India. *All India Rural Debt and Investment Survey 1971-72,* Reserve Bank of India, Vol. II.
3. Johnston, J. *Econometric Methods*, 2nd Edition, Megraw-Hill International Company, 1976.
4. Kendall, M. G. and Stuart, A. *The Advanced Theory of Statistics Vol. 1,* Charles Griffin and Company Limited, London, 1958.
5. Murthy, M. N. *Sampling Theory and Methods*, Statistical Publishing Society, Calcutta, 1977.
6. West Bengal Government. *West Bengal Land Reforms Act (1955)* with amendments upto 1980, Kamal Law House, Calcutta, 1980.
7. *West Bengal* Govt. *District Census Handbook, Nadia 1971.*
8. *A Resume of Agricultural Development in Nadia Krishnanagar,* 1978.

THREE

ASSETS OF THE HOUSEHOLDS

Introduction

All items owned by the household which have money value could be defined as assets of the household[1]. While studying the asset positions of rural households, we accepted this definition and collected the relevant information from the field area. In the context of our study, however a further break up was necessary. We know, the appropriation of economic surplus[2] in the sense of appropriating unearned income is a function of the productive use[3] of the assets of

---

1. This is how the Reserve Bank of India (RBI) defined 'assets' in 'All India Rural Debt & Investment Survey, 1971-72'. The RBI definition, however, excludes crops standing in the fields, currency notes and coins in hand and stocks of commodities (Vol.1, p 11).

2. We do not use the term in the same sense as that of Paul Baran. Instead of defining economic surplus as the difference between actual or potential current output and current consumption, we define it as the difference between aggregate net output and the real income of labour. In this sense, this approximates Marx's notion of surplus value. As a category of income, this is 'unearned income' because labour being the only source of value, the income due to ownership on assets in received without making any contribution to the value of the output. For details of Marx's concept, see [6, chapter 7]. Baran's notion of economic surplus has been discussed in [2, chapter 2].

3. We define 'productive use of surplus' in a very restricted sense. If the owner of the asset uses the asset for furthering the appropriation of unearned income, we call it a productive use of the asset. It should be noted that such an use does not necessarily imply a direct involvement in production on the part of the owner of the asset.

the household. A study on the mode of surplus appropriation and its utilisation should, therefore, seek a further break up of the assets of the household in the line of 'productive' and 'non-productive' or 'income generating' and 'non-income generating' types. Without such a break up, the study on the patterns of surplus use by the rural households would remain perfunctory. Such a differentiation of assets was made on the basis of the use pattern of the same. An asset was considered a productive one when it was used for furthering the generation of income of the household. The alternative use of the asset namely, the use of the asset for the fulfillment of (short period or long period) consumption was considered an unproductive one.

For items like agricultural land or durable household assets where the use patterns of the assets could clearly be identified as income generating or otherwise, such a differentiation could comfortably be made. However, there are certain assets in case of which the productive and unproductive uses overlap, thus making it difficult to get a clear line of differentiation. In such cases, we tried to overcome the difficulty by noting the major use of the asset under consideration and marking it accordingly. For example, building in rural areas is an asset which is used chiefly for dwelling purposes. We have, therefore, placed it in the group of 'non-income generating' assets. By doing so, we had to ignore the occasional use of such assets for income earning purposes. Livestocks, on the other hand, are used mainly for agricultural production. They were, therefore, taken as income earning assets. By classifying 'livestocks' in this way, we ignored the alternative nonproductive use of such assets, e.g., the household consumption of milk and milk products.

The study on the asset positions of the rural households was restricted to the study of the physical assets of the household including inventory in trade. Financial assets including deposits with banks, companies, post offices and cash in hand could not be taken into consideration mainly because of the paucity of data. Not more than 12 per cent of the households supplied any information on such assets, the quality of the data was also poor. The data on gold and jewellery were more perfunctory and we had to drop such items from the purview of our study.

The items included in our study are listed as column elements in table 3.2. Further details about individual elements could be gathered from the questionnaire of the survey (Appendix II).

In the first section of this chapter, we consider the various problems associated with the estimation and valuation of assets. In the second section, we discuss the economic implications of the quantitative information on asset positions of the rural households covered by the survey.

I

It was decided that the volumes of various assets expressed in quantitative terms could be estimated directly or indirectly from the information gathered by interviewing the respondents on the basis of a prepared questionnaire. One weakness of the estimation through interview method, as pointed out by Prof. Mahalanobis, is that it is 'subject to errors of ascertainment arising from the personal bias of the investigators or of the interviewee, or from negligence or wilful distortion of facts by the interviewee' [3, forward, p vi]. Our experience is that the incidence of 'wilful distortion of facts by the interviewee' is very high in case of the quantitative information on the assets collected by interviewing the respondents. This happens because the rural rich, our target population, is always apprehensive about the purpose of a survey on household assets and therefore, they try to suppress facts as far as practicable. As a result, there exists a strong non-sample bias in the form of under reporting in the data collected by this method.

Estimation of owned Land

Since there does not exist any official record in case of most of the assets of the rural households, we could not but depend on the information supplied by the respondents. However, we did not have to follow such an interview method while estimating the most important asset of the rural households, viz., the agricultural land of the respondents. It should be noted that in the original questionnaire, there was no question on the area of agricultural holding owned by the respondents. In fact, the respondents were bypassed while estimating the land of the raiyots. By doing this, we minimised to a large extent, the non-sample bias in the form of under reporting.

Information on the area of agricultural holding owned by the respondents was collected from the Land Records (LR) Department. It is a very old practice of the LR Department to keep records of every parcel of agricultural land of the state on basis of raiyotwari right[4] on land. In order to facilitate such a recording, the district is divided into several settlement circles below which there are revenue *maujas* (the primary units). Maujawise records on every parcel of land were always available and the records were claimed to be foolproof. But there was one problem with such records. The records being *dag* (parcel of land) specific, it was difficult to estimate the number of parcels of land possessed by a specific landowner. One had to go through the records of the numerous parcels of land in a mauja and check every ownership title in order to count the number of the parcels of land owned by a particular landowner in a particular mauja. However, such a difficulty has, of late, been removed by the LR Department itself. During the recent land settlement, the circle offices have been instructed to prepare a single *Khatian* (record of right) for every raiyot in a mauja. In the Khatian, the records of all the parcels of land owned by a particular raiyot in a mauja have been bunched together. By consulting the khatian of a raiyot, one can easily estimate the land officially owned by the raiyot in a mauja.

While estimating the land of a raiyot, we could therefore, venture to bypass him. Only information that we gathered was the names of the maujas in which the raiyot is expected to possess land. From the settlement offices, we then consulted the Khatian book of the relevant maujas and estimated the land of a particular respondent.

Such a method could not, however, take care of the *benami* lands of the landowners. We tried to get a rough estimate of such benami lands by having recourse to listing of probable persons in the names of whom the titles might have been transferred. Local Kanungos helped a lot in apprehending such names. We consulted the Khatian book again and recorded the parcels of land owned by such proxies. Adding the lands officially owned by the raiyots with those in the names of the proxies, we estimate the lands of the respondents.

The estimated land of 136 respondents described in table 3.1 consists of the land owned by the respondent and his associates defined as 'members of the family' of the respondent. The term

---

4. Raiyotwari right is the individual ownership right over a holding. Under such rights the holding is heritable and transferable (see [4], chapter 4).

'family' as considered here, is not restricted to the legal usage of the term[5] as defined under section 14K of the West Bengal Land Reforms Act (1955). Any person taking meals from the kitchen of the respondent or any member in the name of whom the respondent is known to have concealed his land, was considered a member of the family.

Table 3.1: Size Class Distribution of Own Land (136 Households).

Land in Acres	No. of Households
5.01 - 7.50	2 (1.47)
7.51 - 10.00	4 (2.94)
10.01 - 12.50	3 (2.21)
12.51 - 15.00	17 (12.50)
15.01 - 17.50	14 (10.29)
17.51 - 20.00	16 (11.76)
20.01 - 22.50	14 (10.29)
22.51 - 25.00	9 (6.62)
25.01 - 27.50	14 (10.29)
27.51 - 30.00	12 (8.82)
30.01 - 32.50	9 (6.62)
32.51 - 35.00	8 (5.88)
35.01 - Above	14 (10.29)
Total	136

Figure in brackets denote percentages.

Here $\bar{x}$ = 25.54 acres $\bar{x}^*$ = 20.78 acres

s_* = 15.29 acres and s^* = 8.79 acres

*Does not include the highest size class.

About 40 per cent of the respondents included in the study have size of family holdings above 25 acres, the highest amount of land that could legally be possessed by a family in West Bengal. 10.29 per cent of the families have more than 35 acres of land per family. Another 5.88 per cent have per capita holdings in the range of 32.51 acres and 35 acres. The weight of the entries in the higher size classes is very high. This is indirectly established by the fact that the average land per family is reduced to 20.78 acres from 25.54 acres when we exclude the entries in the highest size-class. The elements in the higher size classes, particularly those in the highest size class are also highly dispersed. The standard deviation for the whole series is 15.29 acres. The figure drops to 8.79 acres when we exclude the highest size class.

---

5. See [4], chapter 3.

Table 3.2: Proportion of households reporting and percentage distribution of average value per household of individual items of assets and liabilities as on 30th June 1971 according to area of land owned.

ALL HOUSEHOLDS

Land owned (in acres)	Percentage of households.	Land	Vacant house sites	Buildings	Livestock	Implements & Machine	Durable Household Assets	Financial assets: Shares	Financial assets: Deposits	Dues Receivable: Cash	Dues Receivable: Kind	Total assets
		1	2	3	4	5	6	7	8	9	10	11
Nil	12.48	-	-	14.00	12.76	7.26	41.70	-	24.26	-	-	100.00
00.01 - 00.50	32.98	15.10	0.90	58.11	10.63	2.92	10.67	neg	1.42	0.13	0.112	100.00
00.50 - 01.00	8.41	46.67	0.08	37.12	8.02	2.54	4.94	-	0.58	0.02	-	100.00
01.00 - 1.25	3.19	55.58	0.99	25.73	7.58	2.65	6.69	-	1.66	-	-	100.00
1.25 - 2.50	14.95	62.79	0.18	22.19	6.83	1.58	5.86	0.116	0.42	0.02	0.01	100.00
2.50 - 5.00	14.44	65.81	0.18	18.98	5.41	1.66	6.04	0.08	1.73	0.06	0.02	100.00
5.00 - 7.50	7.71	61.72	1.24	18.35	5.03	2.29	7.20	0.52	3.46	0.11	0.05	100.00
7.50 - 10.00	2.31	70.43	-	16.86	4.94	1.68	4.80	neg	1.11	0.11	0.036	100.00
10.00 - 12.50	2.13	62.33	0.37	17.44	5.60	4.07	6.31	0.02	3.36	0.41	0.074	100.00
12.50 - 15.00	0.61	51.59	2.20	26.55	3.42	3.25	7.22	0.049	5.41	0.31	-	100.00
15.00 - 20.00	0.69	72.22	1.43	16.57	3.55	3.53	1.89	0.05	0.75	-	-	100.00
20.00 - 25.00	0.12	82.65	-	11.19	4.10	0.80	1.24	-	-	-	-	100.00
25.00 - 30.00	-											
30.00 - 50.00	-											
50.00 & above	-											
Total	100.00	60.49	0.60	21.80	5.75	2.35	6.44	0.16	2.25	0.118	0.036	100.00

Source: Prepared on the basis of table 20.24 of All India Rural Debt and Investment Survey, 1971-72.

The valuation of assets

Current market prices in the local areas or any suitable proxy to it was used for evaluating the assets. It should be noted that spatial difference in prices because of market imperfection introduced a bias in the values of the assets, particularly in case of some important assets such as agricultural land, livestocks, etc. Again, the effect of temporal variation in prices on the value of the assets could not be neutralised fully, because all the households were not surveyed on the same date.

Once the physical volumes of the assets were known, various groups of assets were evaluated by various methods. for homestead and agricultural land, the price in the local market was used for evaluating the assets. With respect to pisciculture, poultry and orchard, we used the income capitalisation method. Buildings were evaluated either at original cost minus the depreciation at uniform rate, or at replacement cost at current prices minus depreciation at uniform rate. The latter method was used in case of older buildings, while for the valuation of the newer buildings the former method was retained. For the durable household assets, generally we used the price quoted by the households. When such prices seemed to have large underreporting bias, the assessment of the investigators was used as a better approximation.

For the evaluation of agricultural equipment, we considered the replacement cost rather than the original cost net of depreciation charges of the equipment, because in the world of runaway inflation, the replacement cost seemed to be a better measure of the value of the assets. The depreciation is approximated at a linear rate - the replacement cost minus an estimated salvage or scrap value divided by the estimated life of the equipment, measures the depreciation[6].

More complicated is the problem of measurement of assets in trade, transport and miscellaneous productive activities of the household. There are certain long term fixed assets used for income generating purposes. These are 'stocks' and like any other stock of

---

6. For further details on the evaluation of farm assets, see [1], [5], [8].

assets these could be evaluated by considering the depreciation factor. For example, in case of brick kilns, there are stocks like kiln, chimney, pugmile, spades, etc, which could be evaluated in the same way as in case of other assets. But there are certain assets, short term fixed or circulating type, which can not be measured in the same way as the long term fixed assets because the assets are 'flow type' or dynamic in nature. For example, in case of brick kilns again, there are stocks - in - process, stocks of finished goods, 'receivable' of the producer, stocks of which are continuously changing and, therefore, the measurement of such assets becomes a problem. However, we avoided these intricate problems of accountancy by ignoring the time dimension. The estimated physical asset at the time of meeting the respondent or the stock of 'flowing' asset at a particular point of time was largely used for measuring such assets.

II

The last decennial survey undertaken by the Reserve Bank of India on the debt and investment positions of the households is one of the largest field surveys undertaken in India. It covers over hundred thousand households in the rural areas and about fifty thousand households in the urban areas. In connection with our study, this survey is of great importance because it describes, among other things, the average value per household of individual item of assets (and liabilities) as on 30th June, 1971, for every state and various regions within a state. These data could be utilised for understanding the asset positions of the rural households.

The Debt and Investment Survey (DIS) does not provide us with any data pertaining exclusively to Nadia district. However, the data collected from the region 2 of West Bengal[7] covered some sample households belonging to Nadia district. This, along with the fact that the districts included in region 2 have some features which are common with those of Nadia, justifies the use of these data for developing a preliminary notion on the asset positions of the rural households of the district.

---

7. The districts belonging to the region 2 of West Bengal were West Dinajpur, Malda, Murshidabad, Nadia and Birbhum.

The DIS results: region 2 of West Bengal

The DIS data provide us with the asset positions of rural households on the basis of owned land. The data available are for all households and separately for cultivators[8] and non-cultivators. The landowning households covered in our survey being both cultivators and non-cultivators (i.e., persons practicing absenteeism vis-a-vis production), the primary idea about the asset positions of the target households of our study could be attained by consulting the DIS results pertaining only to all households of the region.

Our table 3.2 has been prepared from the DIS data[9] on the acreage value of individual items of in region 2 of West Bengal. While commenting on the data, we do not find it necessary to develop the wellknown theme of the perverse pattern of the distribution of assets of rural households, because this has little bearing on our study. What we like to focus is that the DIS data confirm the finding of the studies in the Economics of Farm Management (FMS) carried out in some selected areas of West Bengal, that is, agricultural land is the most important asset of the rural households. As table 3.2 indicates, in the region 2 of West Bengal land is, indeed, the major constituent of rural assets for all size classes excepting the lowest two. Not only this. The importance of land in the asset basket of the rural households increases almost monotonically as we move to higher size classes. Machinery and equipments, another group of productive assets, however, behave rather differently. For the lowest size class the percentage of assets in the form of machinery and equipments is the highest (7.26). On the other hand it is a meager 0.80 per cent for the highest size class. There is, however, no indication of an inverse relation between size of holding and the percentage of assets in the form of equipments. The percentage is around 3 and 4 for households with the size of owned land in the range of 10 and 20 acres, whereas the percentage is reduced to 1.58 and 1.66 for households with owned land in the range of 1.25 to 2.50 acres and 2.50 acres to 5 acres respectively.

---

8. A household having an operational holding of area 0.005 acre or above were treated as cultivator household (see [7], Introductory note).

9. Table 3, page 20, 2.3 and 20, 2.4. in [3]

Considering the positions of all the households, it is observed that 21.80 per cent of assets of rural households is in the form of buildings, and durable household assets account for another 6.44 per cent. Thus, on an average, about 28 per cent of rural assets is unproductive or non-income generating type in the form of buildings and durable household assets. The percentage of durable household assets is conspicuously low for the highest two size classes. It remains lower than the average for almost all the households belonging to higher size classes. Assets in the form of buildings also account for lower percentages of total assets for most of the higher size classes compared to the corresponding percentage recorded in lower size classes. Thus, it can not be concluded that the households belonging to higher size classes with respect to the distribution of agricultural land keep higher percentage of assets in the form of buildings and durable household assets.

DIS data do not provide us with the description of the assets of the rural households in allied agricultural activities like pisciculture, poultry and assets in tertiary activities. There are descriptions of financial assets, but the figures are very shaky. For example, it gives a strange information that the households belonging to the highest size class with respect to owned land do not keep any financial asset in the form of shares and deposits and that these households have no dues receivable in the form of cash or kind. So far as the information pertaining to other classes is concerned, no systematic pattern is reflected in the data. The percentage of 'households reporting' being also poor, we do not find it prudent to rely on these data.

In the context of our study, the DIS data, therefore, could be summed up in the following way. It is observed in the first place, that land is the major constituent of rural assets and the importance of land increases systematically as we move to higher size classes with respect to owned land of the households. The distribution of implements and machinery does not follow any systematic pattern. The distribution of non-productive assets in the form of buildings and household durables is not biased in favour of higher size classes. And finally, there exists no clear pattern in the distribution of financial assets, information on which is rather perfunctory.

Asset positions of 136 households of Nadia

Table 3.3 described the asset positions of 136 rural households of Nadia. The assets were divided in two broad groups, namely, income generating and non-income generating types. As in the DIS table, here also, we find that land is the most important income generating asset of the rural households. However, contrary to what we got in case of DIS data, the importance of land as asset of the rural household has a declining tendency as we move to higher size classes. This tendency is not fully captured in the movement of the income generating assets as a whole, because the declining tendency was partly countered by the increasing tendency in the movement of other income generating assets of the households. For example, the share of agricultural equipments and machinery has a definite increasing tendency as we move to higher size classes until we reach the highest two classes where the tendency has been reversed. However, the data definitely indicate that the percentage of non-income generating assets has an increasing tendency as one moves to higher size classes with respect to owned land of the households. This increasing tendency is the resultant of upward movements in the share of every non-income generating asset of the rural households, e.g., building, homestead and durable household assets. Such a systematic tendency is not present in case of any of the income generating assets of the rural households, excluding land in case of which there exists more or less a declining tendency as we move to higher size classes.

One final comment on table 3.3. Assets in the form of allied agricultural activities, agribusiness and other tertiary activities form a very poor percentage of total assets of the rural households in every size class. This indirectly supports the hypothesis that productive use of surplus in non-agricultural activities is very meagre in the rural areas. This is a theme which will subsequently be utilised for developing the central theme of the present study.

Table 3.3: The percentage distribution of the average value of assets per household of the 136 households according to the area of land owned.

Land owned (in acres)	Percentage of households	Homestead[1]	Building	Durable household assets	Total non-income generating assets	Agri. land	Agri. equipments and machinery	Livestocks	Allied agri. activities[2]	Agri. business	Transport	Trade	Misc[3]	Total income generating assets
5.01 - 7.50	1.47	0.76	14.24	4.52	19.52	5.89	1.37	3.21	-	-	-	-	-	80.47
7.51 - 10.00	2.74	0.69	15.57	3.12	19.38	74.22	2.13	4.27	-	-	-	-	-	80.62
10.01 - 12.50	2.21	1.32	12.13	5.31	18.76	73.05	3.01	5.18	-	-	-	-	-	81.24
12.51 - 15.00	12.50	1.42	14.42	6.24	22.08	67.40	3.39	4.21	0.02	-	1.07	1.81	-	77.90
15.01 - 17.50	10.29	2.01	15.76	7.27	25.04	62.90	4.42	3.72	-	0.57	1.84	1.52	-	74.97
17.51 - 20.00	11.76	1.82	14.14	6.65	22.61	68.31	3.52	3.02	-	-	-	0.86	1.67	77.38
20.01 - 22.50	10.29	2.21	16.12	5.82	24.15	66.24	3.17	4.32	-	-	0.78	1.34	-	75.85
22.51 - 25.00	6.62	2.31	15.74	6.32	24.37	67.04	4.46	3.37	-	-	-	0.76	-	75.63
25.01 - 27.50	10.29	1.87	16.26	5.17	23.30	67.26	3.68	3.21	0.01	-	-	0.51	1.82	76.49
27.51 - 30.00	8.82	2.41	16.51	5.21	24.13	69.82	3.06	2.85	0.03	-	-	0.09	-	75.85
30.01 - 32.50	6.62	2.72	15.01	6.71	24.44	70.37	2.74	2.15	0.12	0.17	-	0.02	-	75.85
32.51 - 35.00	5.88	3.02	18.52	7.21	28.75	64.45	2.14	2.25	0.27	0.15	-	1.02	0.97	71.25
35.01 & above	10.29	3.21	17.23	7.52	27.96	65.68	1.92	2.12	0.07	0.21	0.53	1.51	-	72.04

Notes :

1. Includes ponds, orchards, uncultivated land.
2. Pisciculture, poultry.
3. Husking mill, petrol pump, involvement in construction, brick kiln.

For explanation, see text.

REFERENCES

1. Adams, R.L. *Farm Management Crop Manual*, Oxford Book Company, 1953.
2. Baran, Paul. *The Political Economy of Growth*, Pelican, 1973.
3. Govt. of India, *National Sample Survey*, 8th Round, Tables on Land Holdings, No. 66.
4. Govt. of West Bengal, *West Bengal Land Reforms Act (1955)*, Kamal Law House, 1981.
5. Kalhan, A.S. and Singh, Karan. *Economics of Farm Management in India: Theory Practice*, Allied Publishers, 1980.
6. Marx, Karl.*Capital, Vol. 1* Progress Publishers, Moscow.
7. Reserve Bank of India. *All India Rural Debt and Investment Survey 1971-72 Statistical Tables,* Vol. 2.
8. Yang, W.Y. *Methods of Farm Management Investigations*, FAO, Rome, 1965.

FOUR

CLASS DIFFERENTIATION AND ASSET STRUCTURE

Mode of Surplus Use and Assets of the Households

The salient features of a mode of production are made explicit by the features of the associated mode of surplus generation and its utilisation. Every mode of production has certain distinct features of surplus generation and its utilisation; utilisation process differs corresponding to every mode of production just as the generation process differs. As a result, a study on the mode of surplus generation alone fails to unfold the features of a mode of production. Major aspects of the mode of surplus use are to be studied as well, in order to understand the features of a mode of production[1].

The first problem that one faces while taking up an empirical exercise on the mode of surplus use is the problem of measuring what is defined as 'surplus' in Marxian literature[2] . There are difficulties associated with translating the abstract concept of surplus to the arithmetic of quantitative analysis. Consider, for example, the problem of measuring surplus, i.e., surplus value, under capitalism. Surplus in the sense of surplus value being value of a commodity net of constant capital and variable capital concealed in it, in order to

---

1. For an elaboration of this theme, see Introduction of the present volume.

2. 'Surplus' in the sense of 'surplus value' is described in Marx [10, Chapter 7]. For an excellent exposition of the Marxist concept of pre -capitalist surplus, see Hindes, B. and Hirst, P. [11, p 23-28]. Marx & Engels [.12] is, of course, the basic reference.

approximate surplus value, one must estimate value of a commodity, value of constant capital (approximated by the use of fixed capital and other material parts of capital known as circulating capital for each turnover period) and variable capital (value of necessary labour). A quantitative approximation of these categories in value terms is difficult, if not impossible. It boils down to the problem of reducing every category in terms of direct and indirect labour, a suitable approximation of which in value terms seems to be unattainable - there does not exist a satisfactory measure of indirect labour; it is also difficult to measure direct labour because labour is hardly homogeneous. One may recommend a measure in price terms[3]. Such an exercise involving estimation of constant and variable capital in price terms is difficult, particularly with respect to agriculture, where even though capitalism has made some inroad, the accounting system is still at a poor stage of development.

When surplus is conceived as pre-capitalist surplus, the quantitative analysis remains as difficult. The classical essence of pre-capitalist surplus, in the sense of surplus labour is that, in a stagnant economy, the conditions of reproduction of society being not equivalent to conditions of reproduction of labour which remain at the bare minimum, the gap between the two constitutes the social surplus. Since the pre-capitalist surplus does not assume the classical form in a transitional society like that of ours, a direct translation of this concept to the empirical plane is logically impossible. In fact, much of the reality of surplus generation in Indian agriculture betrays a complex combination of 'market' and 'non-market', 'capitalist' and 'pre-capitalist' processes, so much so that any attempt to directly measure surplus by utilizing standard concepts of 'capitalism' or 'pre-capitalism' becomes completely banal in such societies.

We, therefore, feel discouraged in taking up an empirical exercise on the direct measurement of surplus. While looking for a suitable proxy to what we search for, it seems that a spatial and temporal study on the current consumption of non-durables and structure of assets pertaining to the surveyed household, might serve our purpose. Let us elaborate this point. Logically speaking, current surplus in the sense of unearned income[4] is utilised for current con-

---

3. For a method of estimation of constant and variable capital, in the context of Indian industries, see [13].

sumption of non-durables and for asset formation. Assets could again be decomposed into two parts - productive and unproductive assets. Productive assets are income generating type assets. Such assets work as (non-labour) forces of production. Owners of such assets, having power to use or exploit these assets, engage other peoples' labour on these forces of production and appropriate unearned income (in the sense of footnote 4). Thus, he accumulates wealth or increases his surplus. An unproductive assets, on the other hand, may be visualised as investment on durable consumption goods producing services and not income over time. In a sense, the productive asset that increase income, serves the capitalist need of recycling for expanded reproduction. Unproductive assets, in this specific context might broadly be associated with pre-capitalism.

On the basis of this framework, we hold that a study on the mode of surplus use may bypass the problem of directly measuring surplus and considering its behaviour over time, by having resources to measuring current consumption of nondurables and structure of assets (i.e., relative weight of productive and 'unproductive' assets in the basket of assets of a household). An intertemporal behaviour of surplus use could also be studied by considering the time series data on consumption and assets formation. Associated with alternative methods of surplus generation, alternative methods of surplus utilisation could also be identified.

Thus we get a perspective for considering the assets of the households - a general description of which has been given in chapter 3. So far as surplus is utilised for building of productive or unproductive assets, the pattern of surplus use can be approximated by the pattern of asset formation, given the spatial and temporal description of assets of the households.

Limitation of the Classification Scheme of Chapter 3

It might be recalled that in chapter 3, we arranged the assets of the rural households according to the area of land owned by the individual households. The immediate reason for adopting such a classification was to get a general overview of the asset structure of rural households and to compare it with the relevant data of the Debt and

---

4. See footnote 2, Chapter 3.

Investment Survey, 1971-72 (D I S, 1971-72) which follows the same classification scheme[5]. But then, the analytical use of the data arranged in this fashion is limited. It is true that such an arrangement provides one with the opportunity of measuring 'inequality' in asset distribution, the data could also be utilised in making estimates of rural 'poverty' and 'prosperity'; an intertemporal study on the spread of inequality, a standard theme for economic populism, does not also warrant an alteration of the classification scheme[6].

However, a classification scheme followed by the DIS does not address itself to more serious questions regarding 'poverty' and 'prosperity'. The data arranged according to owned land or according to the money value of the assets of the households do not help us understand various dimensions of poverty and prosperity; causal factors behind the existence of poverty for the masses and perpetuation of prosperity for a few, remain also unattended. The empirical study on the complex reality of asset formation and asset expropriation also remains outside the purview of such surveys.

This point should be elaborated. As we have noted above, some assets are productive assets; owners of these assets appropriate unearned income by utilizing these assets. Extending this theme, one may also observe that the extent of poverty and prosperity of a household depends on the volume and the proportion of productive assets in the pool of household assets. Hence, a classification scheme can not provide us with even a primary understanding about the genesis of poverty and prosperity unless we arrange the households on the basis of the relative importance of the productive assets in the total pool of household assets. Again, a study on the various dimensions of poverty and prosperity warrants a further classification of the income generating type assets according to the nature of the productive use of the asset. For example, land, the single most important income generating assets of the rural households, might be used for generating income through pre-capitalist rack renting - arresting overall accumulation and maintaining a pre-capitalist dimension to poverty that may be removed only by removing the monopoly over land by landlords. On the other hand, poverty vis-a-vis land at-

---

5. The DIS (1971-72) also arranges the data by 'size class of money value of assets'.

6. All these could be done provided, of course, we consider all the size-classes, as the DIS (1971-72) does.

tains a capitalist dimension when the landowners generate income by dint of direct and indirect exploitation of wage labour. A classification of households on the basis of size-class of own land or by money value of all assets succeeds to capture this reality only insofar as the 'between type' variation in the behaviour of asset use corresponds to the 'between size-class of land' or 'money value of size-class of asset'. The extent of such a correspondence is not expected to be high, because, a classification by 'size-class of land' or by 'size class of money value of assets' does not, by itself, take care of this dimensional discrepancy.

An alternative classification scheme based on the variation in the nature of surplus use is, therefore, in order. the present chapter is largely devoted to that task.

An Alternative Classification Scheme

For an alternative classification scheme that attempts to differentiate the surplus earning households on the basis of the nature of asset use, it might be advisable to group the households according to their class nature. Since a particular surplus earning class corresponds to a particular mode of production[7], each surplus earning class, in the final analysis, corresponds to a particular mode of surplus generation and its utilisation. If the classes could be identified a priori, the variation in the nature of asset use could also be studied by arranging the data concerning the assets of the households on the basis of the 'type', i.e., 'class' of the concerned household[8].

But how to identify classes, particularly the surplus earning classes? Truly speaking, a class is identified on the basis of the associated mode of surplus generation and its utilisation. We can not, therefore, identify a class, unless we know, a priori, the observed variations in the nature of surplus generation and its utilisation. In

---

7. For example, a capitalist rich peasant represents a capitalist mode of production, a landlord (feudal) represents a feudal mode of production. Difficulties arise with a mixed situation, e.g., semi-feudalism. As we noted in the Introduction of the present volume, there exists a mixed mode known as semi-feudal mode of production. The associated exploiter is 'semi-feudal landlord' or 'semi-feudal rich peasant'.

8. Such a method of analysis belongs to the general orbit of a Marxian analysis. On the relevance of this approach as against the customary 'neoclassical' or 'neo-populist' approach, see [14] and [15].

other words, one can not differentiate classes, unless one could differentiate households on the basis of variations in the modes of surplus generation and its utilisation. Hence, and analysis of the mode of asset use on the basis of an a priori identification of classes, appears to be a logical non sequiter.

There is, however, an escape route. Initially, one may consider one aspect of the mode of production, viz, the mode of surplus generation. Observing the variations in the mode of surplus generation, one may get a primary or tentative grouping or classification of the households. With the help of such a classification again, variations in the nature of surplus use could be studied. Combining these two, one may get a comprehensive class analysis as well as a complete picture of the existing modes of production.

In the remaining portion of the present chapter, we follow this analytical scheme in order to identify the surplus earning classes on the basis of the variations in the mode of surplus generation; the assets of the households have also been arranged on the basis of such a class differentiation in the next chapter.

Surplus Earning Classes in Indian Agriculture

There exist wide differences in the forms of surplus generation among the surplus earning rural households. By identifying such different modes of surplus extraction, one could draw a tentative line of differentiation among these households, first at the theoretical and then at the empirical level. Taking the necessary theoretical clues from Lenin [1] and Mao-Zedong[2], we developed a schematic outline of such an exercise in the introductory part of the present study. In this section, we reopen the issue with a view to developing that outline in some detail. As one might know, Lenin carried out the analysis of rural classes with respect to pre-revolutionary Russia in particular and Europe of the early 20th century in general; Mao-Zedong, on the other hand, discussed it with reference to pre-revolutionary China. Their analyses are commonly held as the theoretical basis of the debate on the question of differentiation among the peasantry[9]. To start with, we, therefore, note the theoreti-

---

9. The first debate on the question of differentiation was in the German Social Democratic Party between Kamtsky and David. Next in line was Russia where Lenin led the debate against the Russian Populists and Mensheviks. Although Kautsky contributed much, Lenin, who led a successful revolution, is considered

cal positions of Lenin and Mao on the differentiation question. We, however, limit our discussion with respect to surplus earning classes only; a discussion on all the classes, particularly on the exploited, has little relevance with respect to the present problematic.

In the context of the European capitalist countries in 1920s, Lenin discussed the following surplus earning classes in agriculture:

(1) The Big Peasants (Grossbauern) or the capitalist entrepreneurs in Agriculture who, as a rule, employ several hired labourers. This class, according to Lenin, also performs manual labour on their farms.

(2) The Big Landowners who directly, or through their tenant farmers, systematically exploit wage labour and neighbouring small (and not infrequently part of the middle) peasantry. One important characteristic of this class is that the members of this class do not engage themselves in manual labour. Although noted as direct discendents of feudal lords, this class in not noted as purely feudal[10]. This class combines rent income and profit income. However, the rent accrued by this class is, in the main, capitalist ground rent because, this rent is categorised as 'indirect exploitation of wage labour'[11]

---

the authority on the peasant question. Mao-Zedong the leader of the Chinese revolution is another important authority, particularly with respect to the peasant question in the Third World countries.

10. When the big landowners are stated to exploit wage-labour (directly and indirectly through tenant farmers), the suggested type of exploitation is nothing but capitalistic. The associated exploiters are, therefore, capitalist exploiters. Lenin, of course, notes that this class also exploits the neighbouring peasantry (both small & middle peasants) over and above the exploitation through wage-labour. Nature of this exploitation is not stated explicitly. If we assume that the exploitation of this category includes some pre-capitalist elements, then this class might be called a mixed class, as suggested by Patnaik [4].

11. Capitalist ground rent is a combination of both absolute and differential ground rent. The differential rent arises from the surplus from the super-profit, that is created by the more productive labour on better soil or on better located plot' [16, p.299]. It is a typically capitalistic phenomenon. Absolute ground rent, which is the claim of the landowner by virtue of legal property right is a legacy of feudalism, Nevertheless, a combination of the two, noted as capitalist ground rent, is nothing but an indirect exploitation of wage-labour. With respect to the component of differential ground rent, which is a surplus from super-profit, this interpretation is obvious. Absolute ground rent under capitalism is also an indirect exploitation of wage-labour, because, 'absolute ground rent is possible only as deduction from the available quantity of value for the benefit of the

What we cull from Lenin is that both the classes, as a rule, exploit wage labour; but while the first type takes part in manual labour, the second does not. This is commonly held as the line of demarcation between these two types of exploiters. The logic for adopting such a a line of demarcation is the following. The Big Landowners do exploit through ground rent, but, strictly speaking, this is also exploitation through wage labour – capitalist ground rent being a part of surplus value only. Hence, the type of exploitation is not qualitatively different from what the Big Peasants practice. However, a rentier should be distinguished from profit earner even under capitalism; in a sense, therefore, the rent exploitation should be mentioned separately and the rentier should be identified separately. At the empirical level, however, the participation in manual labour might serve as a proxy to that insofar as a rent earner abstains from participation in production. It seems that this attribute, i.e., the attribute of non-participation in production, is mentioned by Lenin only in this sense.

In the context of the pre-revolutionary China, Mao-Zedong also identifies two classes of exploiters - viz., Landlord and the Rich Peasant. At the outset, the Landlord in Mao is like the 'Big Landowner' in Lenin 'who does not engage in labour himself' [3, p.137]. But unlike the 'Big Landowner' in Lenin who exploits wage labour, directly or indirectly, the Landlord, as conceived by Mao, does not, in the main, exploit wage labour; he is primarily a rent earner[12], but this rent is not a part of surplus value because the rent is the feudal rent[13]. This phenomenon, i.e., the phenomenon of exploitation through pre-capitalist ground rent, and not the phenomenon of non-participation of the landlord in production, seems to be the differentia specifica for this class in Mao-Zedong.

Apparently, the Maoist concept of a Rich Peasant is the same as 'Grossbauern' in Lenin because, as Mao notes, the main form of ex-

---

landowner, *a deduction from the mass of surplus value*' [16, p.299, emphasis added].

12. 'Collection of land rent is his main form of exploitation' [3, p. 137].

13. That the land rent in China was feudal in character, has been stated by Mao in [2, p. 307, p. 312-13.].

ploitation practiced by this class is the exploitation of wage labour [3, p.138], and like Grossbauern, this class also 'engages in labour himself' [3, p.138]. A deeper investigation, however, indicates that there also exists a serious difference between 'Grossbauern' in Lenin and 'Rich Peasant' in Mao. First, hired labour in China is noted as 'long term labourers' [3, p. 138]. With improper development of labour market, such long term labourers are often unfree[14], thus lacking the quality of wage labour under capitalism. Exploitation in such cases, therefore, bears symptoms of pre-capitalism, even though the phenomenon of buying and selling of labour power has developed to some extent in these economies. Such a form of exploitation by engaging long term unfree labourer is not mentioned in case of 'Grossbauern'. Secondly, alongwith exploitation wage labour, the Rich Peasant in Mao is also mentioned to, exploit other peasants by means of land rent, loan interest or in other ways, [3, p.138]. Compared to exploitation of wage labour, such a form of exploitation was not insignificant in case of the Rich Peasant as the history of the Chinese society indicates[15]. The 'Grossbauern' on the other hand, is not mentioned as being engaged in such a form of exploitation.

On the basis of these observations, it appears that, participation in labour and employment of wage labour are not the chief indicators for Rich Peasants in China, as they had been in case of 'Grossbauern'. A rich peasant in China might combine pre-capitalist forms of exploitation along with the capitalist forms - a practice which we did not encounter in case of 'Grossbauern'. However, such a phenomenon does not rule out, the possibility that there might exist also some rich peasants who were more capitalist than feudal. Because of such complexities, Mao-Zedong was inclined to distinguish between the 'Capitalist Rich Peasants' and 'Rich Peasants of semi-feudal nature'[16], with the observation that 'most of the rich

---

14. For a general description of the working conditions of the Chinese peasantry including the landless who often worked as long term labourers, see [17], [18], [19].

15. See [18], [19].

16. The Chinese Communist Party, while promulgating Agrarian Reform Laws, issued instructions to party workers to distinguish between a 'Capitalist Rich Peasants and rich peasants of semi-feudal nature'. In order to provide the party workers with a guide line for carrying out such a differentiation, a supplementary note with 'How to Analyse Classes' [3] was issued. This supplementary note considers a rich peasant as 'Rich Peasant of semi-landlord nature' (elsewhere

peasants in China are semi-feudal in character' [2, p.323]. The capitalist Rich Peasants, who were small in number, were more of less like 'Grossbauern' whereas the vast majority of the rich peasants were 'Rich Peasants of Semi-Feudal Nature' - a category which has little resemblance with the 'Grossbauern'.

Thus, the Maoist concept of exploiters in Agriculture is substantially different from that of Lenin. A landlord in Mao exploits mainly through pre-capitalist ground rent; a big landowner in Lenin, on the other hand, earns profit as well as capitalist ground rent. A rich peasant in Mao hires outside labour as Grossbauer does. But a rich peasant in Mao may combine pre-capitalist mode of exploitation with the capitalist mode, a Grossbauer, on the other hand, is a capitalist exploiter.

The genesis of such a difference in approach is rather apparent. The difference stems largely from the treatment of ground rent. It is not also difficult to explain the root of the difference in the treatment of ground rent. Lenin was considering the problem of differentiation in the context of a country or a region where capitalism has already established its sway over agriculture so that the character of rent has changed substantially – it has become capitalist ground rent, i.e., a part of surplus value. It need not, therefore, be treated as a separate mode of exploitation. Mao-Zedong, on the other hand, was considering a backward country where capitalism was yet to come in the dominant position. Given improper development of land market, the phenomenon of differential ground rent, that arises out of capitalist competition for control over better soil[17] is seldom present in such societies. Rent is, in the main, an absolute ground rent which arises out of private ownership of land by a small section of feudal

---

called semi-feudal Rich Peasants), 'if the area of land rented out by a rich peasant exceeds in size the land cultivated jointly by himself and by hired labourers' [17, p. 739].

For Mao-Zedong's observation on semi-feudal Rich Peasants, see, for example, 'Request for Opinion on Tactics for Dealing with Rich Peasants in [20, p. 24-25].

Utsa Patnaik, while summarising the Maoist position [4], evidently missed the Maoist line concerning further differentiation among rich peasants. Her line of differentiation in the direction of 'proto-bourgeoisie' (labour hiring greater than rent) and 'proto-feudal' (labour hiring at most as high as rent) and 'proto-feudal (labour hiring at most as high as rent does not follow the Chinese line.

17. See Lenin, [16, p. 297].

proprietors. The exploitation is mainly through rackrenting that becomes possible due to the right of exclusion enjoyed by the landlords. Associated with this, there is usury exploitation effected through an interlinkage between tenancy and credit contracts. Non-market, personalised relations coupled with certain market forces keep the system viable. All these phenomena, which are distinctly different from the nature of exploitation under capitalism, are hardly described in terms of the modus operandi of the exploitation practiced by either the 'Big Landowner' or the 'Grossbauern'. Mao, therefore, introduced two categories, certain attributes of whom were different from those of Big Landowners and Grossbauern.

The Indian case is somewhere between the two. Non-market, personalised relations have, by no means, disappeared. Rackrenting and usury exploitation do exist in rural India. In the rural areas, there exists the vast mass of un – or under – employed who can not emigrate and find jobs outside agriculture; as a result, they exercise upward pressure on rental price of land and downward pressure on wage rate. Again, such a phenomenon gives rise to a situation where extra-economic constraints on tenancy and labour hiring contracts could perpetuate.

However, the situation is not as backward as the pre-revolutionary China. Tenancy of every form is fast declining; a large section of the rural population now depends on wages – so much so that to a large extent the relation of rural rich with the rural poor has became as one of exploition of labour power. There has been a substantial growth in the use of capital inputs such as fertilisers and pump sets. Agricultural production is not as stagnant as it had been before independence. Market forces have developed to a great extent.

As a result, it will be erroneous to analyse the Indian classes in terms of a typical Chinese model. At the same time, a model in terms of direct and indirect exploitation of wage labour alone also fails to capture the intricate reality of exploitation in Indian agriculture. A description that considers both phenomena, might help one understand the reality .

We, therefore, analyse the problem in terms of the following exploiter classes. Corresponding to 'direct and indirect exploitation of wage labour,' which does exist in rural India to a large extent, there might exist two exploiter classes viz., the Big Landowner (in the sense of capitalist landrent earner only) and the capitalist Rich

Peasant (Grossbauern). Corresponding to feudal exploitation, which has by no means disappeared from the countryside, there exist two types of exploiters, viz., the Landlord and the semi-feudal Rich Peasant. Big landowners, according to this categorisation, exploit mainly through capitalist ground rent[18]. The Rich Peasant, on the other hand, exploits the wage labour directly. A rich peasant, because he is a peasant, also participates in production, a non-participant who exploits wage labour directly, belongs to a sub-category that might be called 'the capitalist Rich'. A semi-feudal rich peasant combines both the capitalist and pre-capitalist form of exploitation - no particular form dominates over the other in this case; participation in production is not also ruled out. A landlord is mainly a rent earner - rent being pre-capitalist absolute rent. In order to understand the Indian reality, one should develop an analysis of classes in terms of these categories[19].

Criteria for Empirical Classification

The mapping of such a classification scheme to the empirical world is never trivial. There are several problems that one encounters, while taking up such an empirical exercise. In the context of Indian Agriculture, however, there are two important attempts for finding out criteria for empirical classification of peasantry. We shall consider the exercises first. Our classification scheme will be described next.

For demarcating classes within peasantry at the empirical level, Usta Patnaik proposed a criterion, according to which, the extent of exploiting or being exploited, relative to the extent of self-employment, had been taken as the index of class status within the peasantry [4, 5]. The proposed criterion has been termed as 'labour exploitation criterion' or E-criterion; where E denotes the ratio of outside labour to family labour. According to Patnaik, such an index

---

18. The act of 'direct' exploitation of wage-labour is ruled out in this case. In this sense, it differs from the Leninist concept of 'Big Landowner'. The classification is tentative; we shall elaborate the concept and suggest a change in nomenclature in the next section.

19. This four-class stratification is derived by combining Lenin [1] and Mao [3]. We shall derive a nine-class stratification scheme on the basis of this combination, in the next section.

has its theoretical root in Lenin [1] and Mao [2].

In a critique to Patnaik, Ranjit Sau [9] rightly points out that the E-criterion did not take care of 'dimensional incommensurability' between labour hiring and rent terms in Patnaik's own formulation. His second important criticism was that a simple ratio of 'outside' and 'family labour' misses the co-ordinate of 'surplus product', the fulcrum of Marx's theory of exploitation.

Sau then suggests an alternative criterion for empirical identification of peasant classes. He defines this criterion as the ratio between the surplus product appropriated by the peasant and the surplus product supplied by him. Abbreviated as R-criterion, Sau reduces it to the ratio of surplus product appropriated by household to necessary product. Sau notes it as 'the rate of exploitation' measured in terms of surplus products as against the labour exploitation criterion. He refers Chen. Po-ta [6] in support of his proposed criterion.

In a subsequent rejoinder, Usta Patnaik notes [5] that the suggested R-criterion is not germane to the problem of finding a way of determining the class status of individual households' [5, p. 483]. This is so because, as pointed out by Patnaik, there does not exist any clear correspondence between differing values of the so-called rate of exploitation and differing class-status. 'It is possible for individual members of the same class - agricultural labourer, say - to be empirically subject to differing rates of exploitation; conversely, individual members of differing classes - say poor peasants and labourers - may be subject to the same rate of exploitation' [5, p.483]. According to Patnaik, therefore, the suggested R-criterion is non-sequitur.

Patnaik, however, admits that some of the objections raised by Sau against the suggested E-criterion are well taken. Accordingly, she modifies her original formulation. In place of 'labour use' co-ordinate, she takes up the co-ordinate of surplus product, as proposed by Sau. She also corrects the original formula in order to take care of the problem of dimensional incommensurability.

While appreciating Patnaik's critique of R-criterion, we submit, even the revised E-criterion of Patnaik is open to certain serious criticisms. In the first place, her method simplifies the existing reality by constructing an index in terms of a homogeneous labour. As we note, in the original, as well as in the revised construction, E is measured in terms of 'labour time'. Given improper development of labour market, 'outside labour' is highly heterogeneous in a country like India and therefore, a homogeneous indicator called 'labour time' hardly makes any sense in the context of empirical exercises unless one solves the problem of adding up various types of heterogeneous labour. With respect to Bengal Agriculture particularly, one understands the implication as regards the extent of complications in connection with such an addingup problem, when one notes the extent of variation in the types of labour as identified in [7] and [8]. A simplistic approach like that of Patnaik hardly helps one to understand this reality.

Patnaik took, as Ranjit Sau had taken, the extent of exploitation or being exploited, relative to the extent of self-employment, as 'the single most accurate criterion for differentiation of rural classes' [5, p. 483]. But the class status of a peasant depends not on the extent but on the nature of exploitation. A single index can hardly serve as a scanner for differentiation, because a single index can hardly capture the dimensional differences in the nature of exploitation. The limitation of such an approach becomes apparent while considering the complex reality of a society in transition, where various types of exploitation co-exist. A careful reading of Lenin [1] and Mao [2] reveals that they were aware of such difficulties and therefore, they did not think in terms of a 'single most accurate criterion.'

Usta Patnaik, of course, takes care of the variations in the nature of exploitation. But preoccupied with the problem of constructing 'a single most accurate criterion' so that the extent of exploitation could be measured, Patnaik simplifies the reality of existing variations in the nature of exploitation and gets a simpler problem as regards dimensional incommensurability. She identifies two types of exploitation, viz., the exploitation through rent extraction and the exploitation through extraction of surplus value. She solves the problems of dimensional incommensurability between the two and identifies rural classes accordingly. Thus, in her original formulation,

$$E = [a + b] \div y$$

where 'E' is the index of labour exploitation and 'y' is family labour days in cultivation on the operational holding; 'a' denotes net labour days hired in and 'b' is net labour days taken through rent. Following her approach, the economic class is landlord if $E \rightarrow \alpha$ i.e., if $y=O$. Again, the landlord is a capitalist landlord if, given $y=O$, $a>b$, i.e., labour hiring is greater than rent. The landlord is feudal, if $a \leq b$, i.e., if labour hiring is at most as high as rent. Patnaik takes this approach in the original formulation [4, p. A86-87]. in the revised formulation [5] also, the spirit of the approach remains the same.

A serious reader may find the approach simplistic. Rent extraction is not necessarily feudal, nor the act of labour hiring is necessarily a *sine qua non* of capitalistic exploitation. If the rent is differential rent her criteria fail hopelessly to capture the real nature of exploitation. Similarly 'net labour hiring' does not exclude pre-capitalism because, first, 'hired labour' need not necessarily be 'free labour' in Marxian sense and secondly, even a free purchase and sale of labour power is not necessarily a *sine qua non* for capitalism[20].

Thus, given $y = O$, $E \rightarrow \propto$ may imply 'capitalist landlordism' even if $a < b$ when b is labour days taken chiefly through differential ground rent. Similarly, $a > b$ does not exclude pre-capitalism if labour hiring is hiring of 'long term unfree labour'. Similarly Patnaik's approach of differentiation among rich peasants in the line of 'Proto-bourgeois' and 'Proto-Feudal' Rich Peasant is open to question. It simplifies the existing reality because as in the case of landlordism, it does not take care of the problem of differentiation in the category of 'rent' and 'wages'.

'A single most accurate criterion', like the E or R index that simplifies the existing reality, must not, therefore, be used for empirical identification of rural classes. A suitable composite index that serves as an ideal measure that properly considers both the nature and extent of exploitation pertaining to rural households is not, however, available[21]. As a result, we had to take recourse to what could be called a 'thumb rule' approach , in the line of what had been taken up by the Chinese Communist Party.[22] The following is

---

20. See footnote 3, Introduction, of the present volume.

21. At the time of taking up the empirical exercise on differentiation problem we did not have the opportunity of going through the contributions of Kritsman, Nemchinov and others of the Agrarian section of the Communist Academy of the U.S.S.R. who worked on the empirical problem of differentiation with respect to the Russian data. Some works, particularly that of Nemchinov [21] might have been useful for this exercise.

22. The Chinese Communist Party, in effect, followed a 'thumb rate' approach as evident from 'The Agrarian Reform Law of the People's Republic of China' [17, p. 737]. It is not true that the Chinese Party followed the quantitative method of Chen Po-ta [6] for performing the exercise on the differentiation problem. As we know, Chen Po-ta worked out the average rate of rent exploitation to which households *already grouped into categories* were subject. The question of how to

the outline of the suggested approach.

A primary classification of households could be done on the basis of consideration of exploitation through ground rent. Because of the lack of homogeneity in labour, a direct estimation of exploitation through ground rent in terms of labour time should be avoided. However, area of land leased out may serve as a proxy. Two types of exploiters could be identified in this way; first, the owners of soil who are *predominantly* rent earners[23] and secondly the owners who rent out around half of their lands. The group of rentiers who leasc out less than such a percentage of the soil, have been excluded from this classification scheme, because they are not likely to earn a substantial income from rent. As in case of China, predomination implies the act of leasing out roughly about 3/4 or more of owned land[24]. The estimation is necessarily rough; an accurate quantification is not necessary, nor such a calculation is possible (due to existence of non-legalised tenancy on a large scale).

The owners of soil who are predominantly rent earners are either capitalist ground rent earners or pre-capitalist landlords. The domination of differential rent is the indication of capitalism. But then, it is difficult to distinguish between the two in practice because rent appears, as a combination of differential and absolute ground rent; the two components can not be distinguished because, as pointed out by Kautsky, 'in practice ground rent does not present itself to us divided in parts; it is impossible to say which part is differential rent and which part is absolute rent' (as quoted in [9, p. 298]). One may, however, get an idea about the nature of the rent earners by considering the nature of tenancy contracts in which they operate. Improper development of lease market that thwarts the

---

determine the class status of each individual household and thus *classify* household, i.e., the crux of the present problem, did not concern him.

23. The impoverished widows, minors or very poor persons who do not engage in manual labour and lease out the land, should not be taken in the group.

24. See [17, p.739]. The choice is tentative. The percentage should be such that the return from leased out land is greater than earning from operated land. An equal division of holding might not rule out this inequality because of the possibility of lower productivity in leased out land due to backward technological endowment. (We do not however, hold the view that tenant farming is necessarily inefficient).

capitalist competition for better soil, thus impeding the formation of differential ground rent, might serve as an indirect indication of pre-capitalist landlordism. When the situation is predominantly otherwise, the rent earner is a capitalist rent-earner. It is difficult to translate this theory to an empirical exercise. Some related empirical questions, e.g., the extent of interpersonal variation in tenancy contracts, the extent of adoption of land augmenting technological progress in tenurial holdings, the nature of credit contracts - are to be examined for determining the dominant pattern of tenancy[25].

But then, an enquiry into such questions at most helps one to get an overview about the prevailing tenurial conditions with respect to the surveyed households. It goes without saying that the above mentioned empirical queries hardly help us construct an index for differentiating the lessor households, which is germane to the present enquiry. While searching for a single most effective indicator, we observe that the nature of exploitation, i.e., the type of rent extracted by the big landowners largely depends on the asset base of the associated tenant households. For example, a small lessee whose asset base is weak, usually has poor bargaining power vis-a-vis a big lessor who has definite leverage owing to his superior asset base; as a result, such lessors might develop various patterns of domination and exploitation which assume non-market form; there is hardly an adoption of the new technology on the part of the lessee, there is hardly any intramarginal difference in yield from land; rent, in the main assumes the form of absolute ground rent. A big lessee, on the otherhand, pays a mix of differential and absolute ground rent, the major component of which is the differential rent, because such a lessee usually adopts the land augmenting technological innovations. Seldom the landowner has better bargaining power with respect to these lessee households. As a result, such pattern of domination and exploitation which assume non-market forms are likely to be weak in case of these tenancy contracts.

We, therefore, find it advisable to utilise the 'type of tenancy' for constructing an empirical index for differentiating the lessor households. On the basis of our analysis, it may be suggested that the 'percentage of leasehold lands leased out to small (size of owned land being one hectare to two hectares), marginal (size of owned

---

25. For further details, see Appendix 1 of the present volume.

land not exceeding one hectare) and landless tenants' - might serve as the required scanner. As a tentative approximation, when a lessor household leases out more than fifty per cent of its leasehold land to the small, marginal and landless tenants taken as a whole, the concerned lessor will be classed as a landlord. This lessor is a capitalist rent earner when this ratio is less than fifty per cent.

The households who rent out nearly fifty per cent of their own land are mixed-type households. If the nature of rent be predominantly capitalist, i.e., if the big lessees dominate in the list of lessees, such households are synonymous to 'big landowners' in Lenin, who engage themselves in direct and indirect exploitation of wage labours, provided, of course, the wage labour category is predominantly a category of free labour without extra-economic relations with the employer. Such exploiters will be marked as 'Big Landowner Type 1'. In the absence of exploitation of such a free labour, the exploiter remains a mixed type or a semi-feudal exploiter.

The exploiter is semi-feudal or mixed-type, also when there is the employment of free labour on operated holding and domination of absolute ground rent on the leased out holding. The fourth possible assortment is that both the forms of exploitation is largely pre-capitalist. An exploiter of this category is synonymous to a pre-capitalist landlord. We note this class as 'Big Landowner Type 2'.

For an empirical understanding, one should, therefore, get some indicators for 'few labour'. There might be five different types of labour employed in agriculture, viz., totally unattached labourer, totally attached labourer (farm servant), semi-attached labourers type 1 (attached to an employer for part of the year but free to work for other employers for rest of the year), semi-attached labourers type 2 (obliged to work for the employer whenever called for a stipulated number of days in a stipulated period) and semi-attached labourer type 3 (obliged to work for the employer whenever called for an unstipulated number of days over an indefinite period).[26]. the extent of employment of 'totally unattached labour' might serve as an indicator of the extent of employment of free labour on the operated holding[27].

---

26. See [8]. We do not consider the category of bonded labourer because, the percentage of such a type of labourer might be insignificant in West Bengal, as suggested in [8].

On the basis of this classification of labourers, we note the following. In such cases where there is predomination of capitalist tenancy on leased out land and farm labourer on operated holding is predominately 'totally unattached labourer', the exploiter is the 'big landowner type 1'. In all other cases, the exploiter is mixed type, or semi-feudal exploiter, except in the case of the domination of small lessee on leased out land and that of attached and semi-attached labourer on the operated holding. The exploiter in this case is 'Big Landowner Type 2'. Among the households for whom no significant involvement in leasing out is reported, two types of surplus earning households could be identified. First, there is a section of households for which the employment of totally unattached labour is the dominant feature. Among such households, a section also participates in production. Such households constitute 'capitalist Rich Peasants'. The rest is the 'capitalist Rich' (without the character of a peasant).

In case of the other section of the non-rent earning households, where the attached labourers of various nature dominate, the exploiter is a mixed or semi-capitalist or semi-feudal exploiter, even though the exploitation through absolute ground rent is insignificant in these cases. If the exploiter is also a participant in the labour process, he might be noted as a semi-feudal Rich Peasant. In case of non-participation, the exploiter loses the peasant character. He is then noted as semi-feudal landlord, although he does not lease out his land.

From the four basic classes, we, therefore, identify nine surplus earning strata in the rural India. A summary description and the *difference specific* of each stratum in terms of empirical criteria are given below.

1. *The Landlord*: A landlord is a person who leases out around seventy five per cent of his land. In terms of own land his lessees are mainly small, marginal and landless farmers who account for more than fifty per cent of the leased out land of the landlord.
2. *The Capitalist Rent earner*: A lessor who leases out around seventy five per cent of his land is a capitalist rent earner, if the big farmer (in terms of own land) account for more than fifty per

27. For a quantitative index, we should consider a particular type of labourer as percentage of total direct labour use, both calculated in terms of mandays.

cent of the leased out land of the landlord.

Supplementary Notes: The Landlord and the capitalist rent earner do not usually lease in land. They do not usually participate in production.

3. *The Big Landowner Type 1*: A big landowner of type 1 is a person who leases out around fifty per cent of his owned land and employs wage labour on the rest. More than fifty per cent of the leased out land is cultivated by big farmers. More than fifty per cent of the mandays used in his operated holding is from 'Totally unattached Labour'.
4. *The Semi-feudal Landlord Type 1*: Like a big land owner of type 1, a semi-feudal landlord of type 1 also leases out around half of his land and operates on the rest. More than fifty per cent of his leased out land is operated by the big farmers, but at the same time, the attached or semi-attached labourers account for more than fifty per cent of the employment of mandays on his operated holding. A mixed-type exploiter is a semi-feudal landlord also when the small, marginal and landless farmers account for more than fifty per cent of his leased out land and totally unattached labour account for more than fifty per cent of the mandays used in his operated holding.
5. *The Big Landowner Type 2*: A big landowner of type 2 is a mixed type exploiter like the Big Landowner of Type 1. His leased out land, which is around fifty per cent of his total owned land, is cultivated by tenants; at least fifty per cent of the tenanted land is cultivated by the small, marginal and landless tenants. On the operated land, the employment of attached and semi-attached labour account for more than fifty per cent of total mandays used by the operator.

   Supplementary Note: Exploiters belonging to these three categories may participate in production, but the extent of participation is only marginal. They have no peasant character. These households may also lease in land. But such a phenomenon will be only accidental.
6. *The Capitalist Rich Peasant*: A capitalist rich peasant does not lease out more than twenty five per cent of his owned land. On his operated land, the use of totally unattached labour accounts for more than fifty per cent of the total mandays used by the farm. The owner of the soil also participates in the production.
7. *The Capitalist Rich*: All the attributes of a capitalist rich are the

same as those of a capitalist rich peasant, excepting only one attribute, namely, that a capitalist rich does not participate in production.

8. *The Semi-feudal Rich Peasant*: A semi-feudal rich peasant participates in production. He does not lease out more than twenty five per cent of his land. The use of attached and semi-attached labourers is more than fifty per cent of the labour use on the farm.
9. *The Semi-feudal Landlord Type 2*: I every respect a semi-feudal landlord type 2 is like a semi-feudal rich peasant except the fact that unlike a peasant, a semi-feudal landlord of type 2 does not participate in production.

The associated schematic outline (Table 4.1) might help one in the matter of arranging the relevant data pertaining to a particular surplus earning household and identifying the 'class' of the concerned household.

Surplus Earning Classes in Nadia

Following this analytical scheme, we examined the relevant data pertaining to the sample households of Nadia and classified the surplus earning households according to their class nature. The exercise is tentative; an accurate estimation is not possible due to several weaknesses in the data.

For example, we could not approximate the exact area of land leased out to tenants. As one might agree, even after the 'Operational Barga', tenancy contracts in West Bengal largely retain a non-legalised form[28]. Official data, therefore, underestimate the extent of tenancy. Data collected by canvassing a prepared questionnaire might also suffer from non-sample bias in the nature of under-reporting by the respondents. An exact classification of households on the basis of 'area leased out' is, therefore, difficult, if not impossible.

Because of incomplete information on the area based out, it is quite likely that the list of tenants would also remain incomplete and therefore, one might not get the total picture concerning the area of

---

28. On the limitations of the 'Operation Barga', see [22].

owned land with respect to every tenant household of a respondent. As a result, the percentage of area leased out to 'big' tenants may not also be calculated properly.

Table 4.1: A Schematic Outline on the Differentiation of the Earning Classes.

Serial or code no.of the house-hold	Area leased out as P.C. of total owned land	P.C.of leased out land culti-vated by big farmer*	Imputed mandays of totally unatt-ached labour as P.C. of total mandays**	Whether the owner parti-cipates in production***	The type of Surplus earner
1.	about 75%	less than 50%	not required	not required	Landlord
2.	about 75%	more than 50%	not required	not required	Capitalist rent earner
3.	about 50%	more than 50%	more than 50%	not required	Big Land-owner Type 1
4.	about 50%	more than 50%	less than 50%	not required	Semi-feudal landlord Type 1
5.	about 50%	less than 50%	more than 50%	not required	Semi-feudal landlord Type 1
6.	about 50%	less than 50%	less than 50%	not required	Big landow-ner Type 2
7.	about or less than 25%	not required	more than 50%	participates	Capitalist Rich Peasant
8.	about or less than 25%	not required	more than 50%	does not participate	Capitalist Rich
9.	about or less than 20%	not required	less than 50%	participates	Semi-feudal Rich Peas-ants
10.	about or less than 25%	not required	less than 50%	does not participate	Semi-feudal landlord Type 2.

Notes * In West Bengal it may cover farmer having owned land more than 2 hectares. An index in terms of operated land of the lesse may often be a better alternative.

** includes family labour which might be insignificant in case of surplus earning households. However, unattached labour as p.c. of total outside labour might be a better measure.

*** Participation excludes supervisory activities performed by the landowners.

Again, there are practical problems as regards identification of the types of laboures used by the respondents. We collected data on the employment of attached and semi-attached labourers by the household; the data were not crop-specific, but period-specific. So also was the nature of data concerning the use of family labour, which we collected by canvassing questionnaires. Data on total labour use in terms of mandays were, on the other hand, crop-specific. A direct calculation of the 'percentage of totally unattached labourer' (the residual divided by total labour in terms of mandays) as not, therefore, possible.

Under the circumstances, we had to tackle such problems in such a way that the analysis lost much of its quantitative rigour. Let us explain.

Since the data on 'area leased out' were often unreliable, frequently, we had recourse to an indirect calculation by utilising the data on 'net cropped area' which were more reliable because the respondents usually supply correct information on 'net cropped area', which they consider to be a less sensitive issue. The total arable land, (total agricultural holding net of follow) net of net cropped areas being the net leased out land of household, such calculation might give an indirect estimate of what we search for, provided, of course, the landowner is not cautious enough to over report the 'net cropped area' to balance his under-reporting on 'area leased out'. For such 'cautious' households, who indulge in such an a *priori* calculation, a further check could be performed by considering his net cropped area in terms of 'plough units'[29], reliable data on which are normally available. Comparing the direct information on leased out land with the data derived from such indirect calculation, we estimated tentatively the 'net area leased out' by choosing the highest of the three. Then we calculated the net area leased out as a percentage of total arable land of the household.

But then, an estimation of 'area leased out' through an indirect method debars one from analysing the pattern of owned lands of the associated tenant households, because it does not help one get the direct information on the types of lessees of the respondents. As a

---

29. It is observed that the decision of farmer as regards maintaining the numbers of ploughs (and associated pairs of bullocks) depends on the net cropped area of the farmer. In Nadia, on a average, it was found that a farmer maintains one plough if the net cropped area is roughly one hectare. In our vocabulary, it means that his score is 1 as regards net cropped area in terms of 'Plough units'. Counting the plough units, thus one may get a rough idea about net cropped area of the farmer, provided no tractor is used. (The act of borrowing or hiring of plough from other is not usually found in case of big farmers).

result, the refinements in the analysis of classes according to the type of rent accrued by the respondent could not possibly be achieved. Such a weakness in the data largely explains the reduction of the original nine-class classification scheme to an ad-hoc grouping in terms of four classes. This is an important observation that will be elaborated further when we would explain table 4.4 of this chapter.

The calculation of the percentage of 'totally unattached labourer' employed by a respondent during a calender year was not, however, so difficult. Crop-specific data on labour use being available, we first calculated total farm labourers used by the household during a year for the production of all crops taken together. Total mandays of attached labourers used by the farm has then been imputed by considering the period of attachment of the labourers and by assigning one manday for each day of attachment. Household labour was imputed by assigning one manday for each family labour for each working day during every phase of production of each crop, provided the involvement of family labour had been at the level of participation and not merely at the level of supervision of production.

With these modifications, we take up the relevant data. As outlined in our observations on the methodology of classification, we arranged the households first on the basis of the 'percentage net area leased out'. 52.21 per cent of the households numbering 71 out of 136, were reported to have entered in lease contract as lessors of land. 20 out of 71 have been reported to have leased out around 75 per cent of their individual own lands[30]. 40 out of 71 have been reported to have leased out around 50 per cent of their holding each. For the rest, 11 to be exact, leasing arrangement appears to be insignificant; no household belonging to this category reported to have leased out more than 25 per cent of his land to tenants. The land holding pattern of the households has been described in table 4.2

Information concerning the pattern of owned land of the associated tenants is largely absent in the present set of data because, in larger number of cases, the data on 'area leased out' were calculated by the methods of indirect imputation described earlier. However, we could collect data pertaining to a section of 569 tenants associated with 47 out of 71 lessor households. This was possible be-

---

30. 6 out of 20 cases are found to have leased out 58.21 per cent of own land each, on an average. However, the impression of the investigators being that these households are largely absentee, we have lumped them in this category.

cause the information on tenancy arrangements with respect to these 47 lessor households was collected by the direct enquiry method. Because of several factors including the paucity of fund, we could not observe the asset pattern of all these 569 tenants. But then, a study on a select group of 85 tenants was carried out. It reveals that a typical lessee is either a small or a marginal farmer in the sense that the size of his owned land is either less than 1 hectare or it does not exceed 2 hectares; about 75 of the tenants belong to this category. Of the tenant households, 20 per cent has no land under ownership holding. The percentage of 'medium to big farmer', on the other hand, is conspicuously low. The sample of tenants visited by us is therefore, dominated by landless, marginal and small farmer (table 4.3).

Table 4.2: Size of Owned Land and Typewise Break-up of 71 Reported Lessor Households.

Size of owned land (hectare)	Number of lessors	A	B	C
4 - 4.99	3	0	1	2
5 - 9.99	35	10	20	5
10 - 14.99	23	6	14	3
15 - 19.99	4	2	2	0
20 & above	6	2	3	1
Total	71	20	40	11

Notes A: households who have leased out more than 75 per cent of owned land.
B: households leasing out around 50 per cent of owned land.
C: households leasing out below 25 per cent of owned land.

Although we could not follow any statistically regular process in selecting the tenant housholds[31], we are under the impression that such an observation depicts the representative picture of the district. This view is further corroborated by the estimate of the National Sample Survey which holds that more than 70 per cent of the lessee households in West Bengal are marginal and small farmers (on the basis of owned land), accounting for more than 75 per cent of the area leased in. Thus there exists a strong factual basis as regards the

31. See Appendix 1 of the present volume.

hypothesis that the tenants in Nadia are largely 'small' tenants who usually supply absolute ground rents to their lessor. The incidence of land augmenting technological progress giving rise to differential ground rent might be low in case of such households.

Table 4.3 : Size Class Distribution of Operational Holding and Ownership Holding of 85 Tenant Household.

Size of ownership holding (hectare)	Size of operational holding (hectare) 0.1-0.99	1-1.99	above 2	Total
0	12	1	4	17
0:1 - 0.99	18	19	10	47
1 - 1.99	-	12	5	17
2 and above	-	-	4	4
Total	30	32	23	85

Note : For explanation, see Appendix 1.

This information, however, does not help one in the practical matter of differentiating the landowners, because such information does not suggest that *all* the surplus earners predominantly lease out their lands to the small tenants. If, however, we assume this to be so willy-nilly we ignore the possibility, however, small this might be, of the existence of the capitalist rent earners, the Big Landowners Type 1 and a section of the semi-feudal exploiters who lease out more than 50 per cent of their holdings to 'big' tenants.

We, therefore, refrain from pursuing the classification on the basis of the hypothesis that most of the tenants belonging to *every* lessor, are small tenants. With respect to the present set of data, such an analysis would have been over ambitious. Rather, we find it advisable to recognise that, a further classification of households on the basis of nature of tenancy contracts is not possible because of the weakness of the present data. Thus, one cannot differentiate between a landlord and a capitalist rich on the basis of these data. The differentiation between a big landowner of type 1 and a big landowner of type 2 and a semi-feudal exploiter should not also be attempted.

Willy-nilly, we, therefore, had recourse to lumping all the households leasing out more than 75 per cent of the own land in a single class. In order to note that no further refinement was attempted, we assign this group a new name, viz., 'the Absentee'. The selection of the nomenclature has largely been guided by fact that this class usually abstains from production. They are largely owners but not operators. An 'absentee' household, according to this classification is either a landlord or a capitalist rent earner. However, the general trend being that the tenants are usually 'small' in terms of owned land, we may suggest that the predominant element in the class of 'the Absentee' is the element of landlordism (in the pre-capitalist sense, i.e., our category 1 in table 4.1).

Similarly, the four classes leasing out around fifty per cent of holding, cannot be subdivided further in terms of three different categories. An ad hoc classification, by lumping all these classes together, was attempted. We noted this lumped class as 'the semi-absentee'. The selection of nomenclature was influenced by the consideration of similar nature as had been taken into account in case of 'the Absentee'. A semi-absentee is only partially absent from production. He operates in one half of his land. A semi-absentee may not be a pre-capitalist exploiter as an absentee usually is. He may combine both the capitalist and pre-capitalist methods of exploitation and possibly no element dominates in his method of surplus extraction.[32] Even if his tenants be by and large 'small', his exploitation may not be totally pre-capitalistic in nature because, in that case, the totally unattached labour might dominate in the component of labour use in his operational holding.

Utilising the labour use component and the information on the nature of participation of landowner in the production process, we considered the possibility of the existence of the last four classes described in table 4.1. It was observed that there did not exist any respondent who does participate in production and, at the same time employs 'totally unattached labourer' to an extent which is less than fifty per cent of the labour use on the farm land. In other words, the category of the semi-feudal Rich Peasant was not present in the field area. There were, however, 5 elements in the set of the semi-feudal Rich. The number of elements in this set being so small (only about 3 per cent of the total number of household), in this analysis, we did not find it necessary to study the behaviour of this class separately. Instead, we lumped this class with the 'semi-absentee'. The reason

---

32. In this sense, this class is the same as the 'Landlord' in Rudra [23].

for lumping this class with the 'semi-absentee' in that this class is not exactly a capitalist class, because the wage labour is predominantly 'unfree'; on the other hand, it is not also exactly a pre-capitalist class, because it employs wage labour, and earns some sort of a profit income. Such a half way position of this class warrants lumping it with no other but the 'semi-absentee' class.

Table 4.4: Typewise and Zonewise Distribution of Big Ryots Nadia.

Zone	Type		Rich Farmer		Total
	Absentee	Semi-absentee	Participating	Non-participating	
Advanced	9(17.31) (33.33)	18(34.62) (41.86)	21(40.36) (36.84)	4(7.69) (36.36)	52(100.00) (37.68)
Moderate	9(21.43) (33.33)	11(26.19) (25.58)	20(47.62) (35.09)	2(4.76) (18.18)	42(100.00) (30.43)
Backward	9(20.45) (33.33)	14(31.82) (32.56)	16(36.36) (28.07)	5(11.36) (45.45)	44(100.00) (31.88)
Total	27(19.57) (100.00)	43(31.16) (100.00)	57(41.30) (100.00)	11(7.97) (100.00)	138(100.00) (100.00)

Note: For explanation of 'zones', see chapter 2. Row-wise percentage is that of total in a zone. Co'oumn-wise percentage is that of total of a 'type'. For explanation, see the text.

A large number of households belonged to the category of capitalist Rich Peasant. A small but significant proportion was also the capitalist Rich. The difference between the two, as we have observed, is that the Capitalist Rich does not participate in production, whereas the capitalist Rich Peasant does. Both, however, employ outside unattached labourers to a large scale (more than 50 per cent of the total labour use). This similarity might be noted by denoting both of them as 'Capitalist Farmer,' or to follow common usage, 'Rich Farmer'. However, the point of difference is more important. The important distinction between the two is that a rich peasant is an enterprising type producer who engages himself in the production; on that score, the capitalist Rich is non-enterprising. One may, therefore, note the classes as the 'participating' or 'enterprising rich peasants' and 'the rich of non-participating' or 'non-enterprising nature' respectively.

Table 4.4 describes the type wise and zonewise distribution of Big Ryots of Nadia to the extent the variation in 'type' of surplus earner could be captured in terms of this revised classification scheme. As the table indicates, 19.57 per cent of the landowners belongs to the 'Absentee' category. 31.16 per cent belongs to the category of 'semi-absentee' households. The rest, about 50 percent of the households belongs to the category of Rich farmers, 83.82 per cent of which is 'participating type', the rest is 'non-participating'.

About zonewise break up, one interesting observation is that the participating rich farmer is the single most dominant type landowner in every zone. Semi-absentee is the next important group. Typewise distribution among zones, however, indicates that the 'Absentee' households are distributed evenly among the three zones. Most of the rich farmers, on the other hand, belong to the advanced zone. However, no statistically significant association between 'types' and 'zones' is indicated (table 4.5).

Table 4.5 : Measures of Association

Attributes	Value of contingency	Degree of freedom	Comment
Zonewise and type wise break up	1.38	4*	80 to 90 per cent probability of being excluded in the sample
Backward zone Absentee	0.032	1*	80 to 90 per cent and probability of being excluded in the sample
Advanced zone Rich Farmer	0.048	1*	80 to 90 per cent and probability of being excluded in the sample

Note: Data do not consider further break up of rich farmers. Hence the degree of freedom has been reduced by 1.

With such a classification of households, we shall now consider the spatial and temporal distribution of the assets of the surveyed households in the subsequent chapters.

REFERENCES

1. Lenin, V. I. Preliminary Draft Theses on the Agrarian Question, *Collected Works*, Vol. 31, Progress Publishers, Moscow, 1974.
2. Mao Zedong. Chinese Revolution and Chinese Communist Party, *Selected Works*, Vol.2. Peking, 1977
3. ——— How to Differentiate Classes in Chinese Society, *Selected Work*, Vol. 1, Peking, 1977.
4. ——— Patnaik, U. Class Differentiation within the Peasantry, *Economic and Political Weekly*, Vol. XI, No. 39.
5. ——— Empirical Identification of Peasant Classes Revisited, *Economic and Political Weekly*, Vol. XV, No. 9.
6. Chen Po-ta. *Study of Land Rent in Pre-Liberation China,* Peking, 1956.
7. Rudra, A. The Self-contained Village Society, *Frontier,* Calcutta, January, 1981.
8. Bardhan, P. & Rudra, A. Types of Labour Attachment in Agriculture, *Economic and Political Weekly*,Vol. XV, No. 35.
9. Sau, R. A Theory of Rent and Agrarian Relations, *Economic and Political Weekly,* Vol. XIV, No. 26.
10. Marx, K. *Capital*, Vol. 1, Progress Publishes, Moscow, 1967.
11. Hindes, B. and Hirst, P. Pre-capitalist Modes of Production, Routledge and Kegan Paul, London, 1975.
12. Marx, K. & Engels, F. *Pre-capitalist Socio-Economic Formations,* Progress, Publishers, Moscow. 1979.
13. Khasnobis, R. and Nath, N. Accumulation of Capital & Share of Wages in Indian Industries: A case study, *Business Studies,* Vol. IV, No. 1, Calcutta,
14. Bharadwaj, K. *On some Issues of Method in the Analysis of Social Changes,* University of Mysore,1980.
15. Greene, F. and Nore P. (ed.) *Economics : An Anti-Text.* Macmillan Press, 1977.
16. Lenin, V. 1. The Agrarian Programme of Social Democracy in the First Russian Revolution. *Collected Works,* Vol. 13, Progress Publisher, Moscow.
17. Hinton William. *Fanshen,* Penguin, 1972.
18. Belden Jack. *China Shakes the World,* Pelican, 1973.
19. Moore Barrington Jr. *Social Origins of Dictatorship and Democracy,* Penguin, 1969.
20. Mao Zedong. *Selected Works,* Vol. 5, Peking, 1977.
21. Shanin, T. Measuring Peasant Capitalism, *Peasants in History*. edited by Hobsbwam, E. J. and others, Oxford University Press, 1980.
22. Khansnobis, R. Operation Barga : Limits to Social Democratic Reformism, *Economic and Political Weekly,* Vol. XVI, No. 25-26.
23. Rudra, A. Class Relations in Indian Agriculture - I,II,III, *Economic and Political Weekly,* June, 1978. .

FIVE

ASSET STRUCTURE AND THE MODES OF SURPLUS USE

Introduction

In chapter 3, we presented a broad outline of the asset structure of the surveyed households. Households had been classified there according to the size of land owned by the individual households. We have already noted that such an analysis reveals the observable variations in the asset structure only to the extent the 'between type', i.e., 'between class' variation in asset structure is captured in this classification, because, the pattern of assets is largely determined by the class position of an individual. Since there is no reason to suppose that a reasonable correspondence between groups according to the area of owned land and those according to the class nature of a household exists, the extent of such a conformity might be very poor.

With a view to overcoming this difficulty, in Chapter 4, we have developed a scheme for an *a priori* classification of the households according to the nature of exploitation they practice, and have arranged the sample households accordingly (See table 4.4). In this chapter, we utilise this classification scheme and attempt to analyse the variation in the asset structure among different surplus earning classes.

The variation in the asset structure reflects the variation in the pattern of surplus use in as much as the surplus is utilised for the formation of productive and unproductive assets of the households. After analysing the pattern of variation in asset structure, we have, therefore, attempted to study the variation in the pattern of surplus use, so far as such a phenomenon was reflected in the data on assets of the households. Needless to say, such an analysis is mostly indicative in nature.

As in Chapter 3, assets have broadly been divided here in two groups, viz., 'income generating' and 'non-income generating'. The rationale of such a differentiation and the method of grouping various assets in these two groups, have already been discussed. While 'homestead', 'building', 'durable household assets' have been grouped as 'non-income generating type', 'agricultural land', 'farm implements', 'livestock', 'agri-business', 'transport', 'trade' and 'allied agricultural activities' have been lumped together as 'income generating' or 'productive assets'. Data do not include financial assets in the form of 'deposits with banks, companies, post offices', 'cash in hand' and 'informal financial assets' in the form of fund in usury[1], due to paucity of realiable information.

Assets have been aggregated in terms of prices in 1980- the year of canvassing the questionnaire. For most of the items of assets, the information was collected in terms of physical units. The average market price per unit of the relevant assets was collected separately and the valuations were done accordingly. In case of some items (e.g., the household durables) only the notional values were available. We accepted them, unless if they seemed to have large bias in the form of under-reporting. Notional assessments of the investigators were used in such cases of under-reporting, as proxies (Investigators were instructed to use separate note sheet, if necessary, to supply his own assessment).

Variation in Owned hand

It might be recalled that out of 138 households, we have information on owned land in case of 136.[2]

---

1. It is well known that the acquisition of informal financial assets is normally grossly underreported. Debt to informal credit agencies is, however, expected to be reported more accurately. Had it been possible to approach the households that had debt bondage with the big land owners of the present survey, we might have been able to estimate the financial assets in the form of usury. However, such an exercise could be undertaken with respect to a sample of 85 tenants households (See appendix 3) associated with only 45 landowners. The sample being very small, no generalisation was attempted.

2. See Chapter, 2, page 16.

Table 5.1 describes size distribution of owned land of these reported households, grouped in three surplus earning classes, namely, 'absentee', 'semi-absentee' and 'rich farmers'. Average per capita holding for all these households in 26.33 acres. Typewise distribution indicates that the average is the highest for the semi-absentee class. It also shows that the smallest is that of the rich farmer. The variation is also quite high. The average varies from 22.65 acres to 31.22 acres. On an average, a semi-absentee household has 3.27 acres of land more than that of the absentee; compared to the rich, on an average the semi-absentee enjoys 8.57 more acres. Thus it seems logical to conclude that, on the basis of owned land, the semi-absentee is the most powerful group of surplus earners in rural Nadia.

Table 5.1 : Typewise Size Class Distribution of Own Land (136 Households)

	X_A	X_{SA}	X_R
Land in Acres	Absentee	Semi absentee	Rich
05.01 – 07.50	-	-	2
07.51 – 10.00	-	1	3
10.01 – 12.50	-	-	3
12.51 – 15.00	-	4	13
15.01 – 17.50	2	4	8
17.51 – 20.00	5	4	7
20.01 – 22.50	3	7	4
22.51 – 25.00	3	3	3
25.01 – 27.50	1	7	6
27.51 – 30.00	2	2	8
30.01 – 32.50	3	2	4
32.51 – 35.00	2	3	3
35.01 – Above	4	6	4
Total	25	43	68

	X_A	X_{SA}	X_R
Mean	27.95 (24.10)	31.22 (21.04)	22.65 (20.03)
Standard Deviation	10.85 (05.67)	18.47 (09.36)	13.95 (07.45)

Figures in the perenthesis exclude open class.

We did not perform test on the difference between means & s.d.s, because of the objections rightly raised by Rudra (1, p.303) with respect to parametric tests.

The semi-absentee is, indeed, the most powerful group in rural Nadia in terms of total assets per household. We shall try to establish this point presently. However, a closer scrutiny disproves the claim that they are the most powerful group in terms of the average *area of land owned by the households. Table 5.1 includes an open ended class where there exist some abnormally high entries. If we drop this class, the dispersion registers a sharp decline (about 50 per cent) in case of all the surplus earning groups. The openended class has therefore inputed a strong upward swing in the description. However, the swing is not uniform across the surplus earning groups. If we drop the open class, on the one hand, the average area of owned land for the semi-absentee is reduced by as high as 10.18 acres; those of the absentee and the rich, on the other hand, are reduced only by 3.85 acres and 2.62 acres respectively. As a result, the previous ranking is changed. The absentee emerges as the most powerful class on the basis of the area of owned land. The semi-absentee ranks second, closely followed by the group of rich farmers, the average size of whose holdings is just 1.01 acres lower than that of the semi-absentee.

In table 5.1, we did not consider the typewise distribution of 68 rich peasants according to the area of owned land. We take up this issue in the next table which shows that there are 11 'operating and not participating' type rich farmers. Average area of owned land per family is 18.52 acres in this group. While no family holds more than 30 acres of land, each family has more than 10 acres of own land.

The overwhelming majority of these rich peasants are 'operating and participating' type. They have 23.44 acres of land on an average. 4 members hold more than 35 acres each. Excluding them, the average in 20.03 acres. There exists considerable dispersion in the data largely due to abnormal entries in the open class. If we exclude the open class, the dispersion is reduced by about 50 per cent. The average size of holding is still higher than that of the other group of rich farmers. So far as the area of owned land serves as an indicator of rural power, 'operating and participating' type rich farmers are thus more powerful than 'operating and not participating' type rich farmers.

Table 5.2 : Typewise Distribution of 68 Rich Peasants with Respect to Own Land

Own land in acres	Operating and not Participating (Xon)	Operating and participating (Xop)
05.01 – 07.50	..	2
07.51 – 10.00	-	3
10.01 – 12.50	1	2
12.51 – 15.00	3	10
15.01 – 17.50	1	7
17.51 – 20.00	3	4
20.01 – 22.50	1	3
22.51 – 25.00	-	3
25.01 – 27.50	-	6
27.51 – 30.00	2	6
30.01 – 32.50	-	4
32.51 – 35.00	-	3
35.01 – Above	-	4
Total	11	57

	X_{ON}	X_{OP}
Mean	18.52	23.44 (20.03)
Standard Deviation	05.58	14.91 (07.45)

Figures in the parenthesis exclude open class.

The zonewise distribution of owned land indicates (table 5.3) that the zonewise variation in average owned land is not very high. The two way classification, however, indicates that the semi-absentee households have the highest per capita holding in both advanced and moderate zones. In the backward zone, on the other hand, the 'absentee' households surpass others. No overall association is, however, indicated, because the co-efficient of contingency and the associated χ^2 value are conspicuously low.

Productive and Unproductive Assets of the Households: Some Preliminary Observations

A quantitative estimate of the average value of total assets per household indicates (table 5.4) that the semi-absentee has an asset base which is about 20 per cent higher than that of the absentee. The average value of total assets per household for the rich is 52 per cent lower than that of a typical semi-absentee. In terms of total assets therefore, the semi-absentee is the most powerful class in the rural areas. The observation remains valid even if we exclude the open class.[3]

Table 5.3: Zonewise abd Typewise Distribution of Own Land (Mean in Acres)

Type/ Zones	Absentee	Semi-absentee	Rich	Mean of Zone
Advanced	23.38	32.01	23.55	25.90 (20.45)*
Moderate	27.08	25.57	22.55	24.29 (21.85)*
Backward	32.36	29.29	21.73	26.85 (22.18)*
Mean of Type	27.95 (24.10)*	31.22 (21.04)*	22.65 (20.03)*	26.33 (21.04)*

Coefficient of contingency = 0.054
χ^2_4 = 1.425
Note : * excluding the open class

In contingency table, we considered all the values, including 14 cases belonging to the open class.

Table 5.4 also indicates that the assets of the respondents are mostly of productive type . Thus, about 80 per cent of the assets of the semi-absentee is productive in nature. The relevant percentage is almost the same for the rich. The percentage is 74.41 for the absentee class. This is lower than that of the other two groups; but, the percentage *per se*, is quite high.

The description of the money value of assets reveals that all the households under observation belong to the Rs. 1,00,000 and above, i.e., the highest asset group of the Debt and Investment Survey (DIS), 1971. A comparison with the DIS data indicates that even excluding 'Financial assets' and 'Dues receivable' which had not been covered in our survey, the average value of each group is substantially higher than that of the highest asset group for 'cultivators' in

---

3. The average value of total assets (rupees in 1980) per household excluding the open class is as follows.
Absentee Rs. 270321.51
Semi-Absentee Rs. 291565.74.
Rich Farmer Rs. 22410767

RBI study for West Bengal [2, p. 133]. A comparison with relevant data for region 2 of West Bengal (to which our district belongs) further reveals that the households under examination belong to a size class in which, the number of households reporting is nil according to the RBI estimate [3, 20.2.8]

Table 5.4: Typewise Distribution of Average Value (Rupees in 1980) Per Household of Productive & Unproductive Assets

Type of Household	Value of Productive Assets	Value of Unproductive Assets	Total Assets
Absentee	229427.51	78951.33	308328.84
	(74.41)	(25.60)	(100.00)
Semi-absentee	312064.30	75671.24	387705.68
	(80.49)	(19.52)	(100.00)
Rich	207157.37	47937.20	255067.57
	(81.22)	(18.79)	(100.00)

Note: Row-wise additions differ marginally from total values of Assets due to rounding off at various stages of computation.

Such a discrepancy is largely due to the difference in sample frame. It might be recalled that the RBI study is village specific at the first stage. As a result, it considers big land-owners only to the extent they appear in a 'typical' village.[4] In a sense it is a restricted survey, because it studies the phenomenon so far as it appears in a village typical not in the sense that it includes more substantive households, but typical in the sense of footnote 4. A big landowner specific survey, on the other hand, goes beyond this village specificity and considers 'typical' big land-owner so far as it appears in the region, not only 'typical' but also in non-typical villages. Such a study, therefore, captures more substantive households better than the village specific surveys do.

The Productive Assets

Our study conforms to the common wisdom that land is the most

4. RBI selection was based on geographical and demographic (inclusive percentage of agricultural population) factors. [See 2, p.5 and 6].. Needless to say, it did not consider percentage of substantive farmers as one of the attributes of a typical village.

important asset in the rural areas. In case of the observed households, 70 to 80 per cent of total assets is in the form of land. As percentage of productive assets, the importance of land is still higher, In fact, 80 to 97 per cent of productive assets is in the form of land (table 5.5) A classwise break up reveals that the rich farmers keep 87.47 per cent of their productive assets in the form of land. For the semi-absentee, the percentage is 80.03. The absentee, on the other hand, keeps almost all his productive assets in the form of land - 97.53 per cent of his productive assets is land (table 5.5).

Since productive assets generate surplus, data indicate that land is the most important means of surplus generation (and exploitation) in the rural areas. However, the importance of land as means of exploitation is the highest for the absentee. They exploit almost entirely through land. Others have diversified a bit. About 20 per cent of the productive assets of a semi-absentee household and 12.53 per cent of productive assets of rich household are retained in non-land form.

Itemwise break up indicates that about 7 per cent of the productive assets of the semi-absentee households is in agriculture in the form of farm implements and livestock. The rest, about 12.70 per cent, is in trade, transport, agribusiness and other tertiary activities. In quantitative terms, out of productive assets worth of Rs. 312064 per family, about Rs. 40,000 is invested in non-agricultural,tertiary activities.

A rich farmer invests about 11 per cent of his productive assets in the form of farm implements and livestock, leaving only about 1 per cent for investment in tertiary activities. Productive assets of this class is thus heavily tilted in favour of the primary sector.

Diversification in the form of assets outside agriculture, teritiary sector to be precise, is undertaken largely by the semi-absentee class. For a scrutiny of table 5.5, one gathers that 95.42 per cent of total assets outside agriculture belongs to the semi-absentee. The rest, only about 4.57 per cent is accounted for by the rich and the absentee.

However, the phenomenon of asset formation outside agriculture need not be overemphasized. Only about 5 per cent of total assets of the households belongs to tertiary sector. This indirectly supports the hypothesis that productive use of surplus in non-agricultural activities is generally low in case of the observed households, inspite of the fact that a class of surplus users are trying to divert their assets to tertiary activities.

Table 5.5 : Typewise Distribution of Average Value (Rupees in 1980) Per Household of Individual Items of Productive Assets

Type of Household	Agrl. land	Agrl.equipment & machinery	Live stock	Allied Ag.Activities	Agri. Business	Transport	Trade	Misc. Activities	Total Productive Assets
Absentee	223754.17	61.67	5303.25	92.50	30.74	185.18	-	-	229427.51
p.c. of Total Assets*	72.57	0.02	1.72	0.03	0.01	0.06	-	-	74.41
p.c. of Productive Assets*	97.53	0.03	2.31	0.04	0.01	0.08	-	-	100.00
Semi-absentee	249760.00	9925.26	12445.35	271.40	2016.06	10623.14	13802.32	13220.76	312064.30
p.c. of Total Assets*	64.42	2.56	3.21	0.07	0.52	2.74	3.56	3.41	80.49
p.c. of Productive Assets*	80.03	3.18	3.99	0.09	0.64	3.40	4.42	4.24	100.00
Rich	181211.00	12355.27	11539.05	949.75	795.71	229.41	92.05	-	207157.37
p.c. of Total Assets*	71.04	4.84	4.52	0.37	0.31	0.09	0.04	-	81.22
p.c. of Productive Assets*	87.47	5.96	5.57	0.46	0.38	0.11	0.04	-	100.00

Notes : * Refers to that of the type of household.
For explanation of individual items, see chapter 3.
Row-wise additions differ marginally from totals due to rounding off at various states of computation.
For explanation of variations of quantitative values, see the text.

Non-productive Assets

Non-productive assets are largely in the form of buildings (table 5.6). Thus, the absentee households maintain 62.41 per cent of the non-productive assets in the form of buildings. The percentages are 70.09 and 75.08 for the semi-absentee and the rich respectively. As a percentage of total unproductive assets, the share of 'buildings' is the highest for the rich and the lowest for the absentee. However, the position changes, if we consider the shares as proportions of total assets. The Absentee keeps about 16 per cent of total assets on 'buildings'; while the Rich and the Semi-absentee retain 14.11 and 13.68 per cent of total assets in the form of buildings.

Table 5.6: Typewise Distribution of Average Value (Rupees in 1980) Per Household of Individual Items of Non productive Assets.

Type of Household	Homestead	Building	Durable Household assets	Total
Absentee	6875.73	49270.43	22528.00	78951.33
p.c.of Total Assets*	2.23	15.98	7.31	25.52
p.c.of Unproductive Assets*	8.70	62.41	28.53	100.00
Semi-absentee	3935.82	53038.04	18697.38	75671.24
p.c.of Total Assets*	1.01	13.68	4.82	19.51
p.c.of Unproductive Assets*	5.20	70.09	24.71	100.00
Rich	2678.21	35990.03	9268.95	47937.20
p.c.of Total Assets*	1.05	14.11	3.63	18.79
p.c.of Unproductive Assets*	5.59	75.08	19.36	100.00

Notes: * Refers to that of the type of households.
For explanation of individual items, see chapter 3.

Both in absolute and relative terms, an absentee household has more durable assets than other households. So also is the position with respect to the homestead. The over-all picture (last column of table 5.6) is that an absentee household keeps 25.52 per cent of total assets as unproductive assets. This is higher than those of other two groups, between which, however, the difference in this respect is small.

In terms of unproductive assets, therefore, the absentee scores higher than other two classes. The absentee keeps the unproductive assets mostly in the form of buildings and durable household assets. They keep a small proportion of total assets in the form of homestead.

Variation in Asset Structure and Modes of Surplus Use

So far as the surplus is utilised for building of productive or unproductive assets, the pattern of surplus use can be approximated by studying the pattern of assets formation. In this section we describe the assets structure of the households. On the basis of such a discussion, we attempt to work out the pattern of surplus use, so far as the pattern is reflected in the asset structure of the households.

There are three surplus earning classes that we have identified. We discuss the asset structure of these three classes separately because such a presentation lays bare the *differentia specificia* with respect to asset structure of the surplus earning classes more distinctly.

We have utilised such a discussion for developing an exercise on the patterns of surplus use, too;. However, such an exercise could be developed only to the extent the patterns are reflected through the asset structure of the surveyed households. This discussion is more or less indicative in nature.

The absentee : An absentee household keeps, on an average, three fourth of its assets in the productive form, 97.53 per cent of which is in the form of agricultural land. Land is thus the most important means of surplus generation for this class. But, as we gather from the relevant table (5.5), it keeps very little agricultural equipment. In fact, 70 per cent of the absentee does not keep any farm implement (table 5.7). Even for such absentee households which have reported to possess farm implements, the average value of such assets is only Rs. 208.14. This indicates that the agricultural implements possessed by the absentee are traditional in nature. No such household possesses tractor or modern farm implements. This observation is consistent with the view that, in the main, the absentee represents rentier interest and they do not utilise the surplus for asset formation in the form of farm implement.

Only 3 out of the 27 households invest in allied agricultural activities. No household has involvement in trade or miscellaneous agricultural activities. There is only one household that invests in agri-business. One absentee household has marginal[5] involvement in transport business. The overall picture is such that a negligible per centage (about 0.32) of total estimated assets of the households in the tertiary sector is reported to be with the absentee class.

An absentee keeps about one fourth of his total assets in the form of unproductive assets. Most of such assets are in the form of buildings and consumer durables. Compared to other surplus earning classes, this class has a definite tilt in favour of non-productive assets.

Table 5.7: Number of Households Reporting and the Average Value (Rupees in 1980) Per Reported Household of Some Selected Individual Items of Productive Assets.

	Farm Imple-ment	Allied Agri. Activities	Agri. Business	Transport	Trade	Misc.
Absentee						
Average value of the group (Rs)	61.67	92.50	30.74	185.18	-	-
No. of households reporting	8(29.6)	3(11.11)	1(3.70)	1(3.70)	-	-
Average value per reported household (Rs)	208.14	832.50	830.00	5000.00	-	-
Semi-absentee						
Average value of the Group (Rs)	9925.26	271.40	2016.06	10623.14	13802.32	13220.76
No. of households reporting	43(100.00)	11(25.58)	21(48.84)	9(21.0)	36(83.72)	6(13.95)
Average value per reported household (Rs)	9925.26	1060.93	4128.12	50755.00	16486.10	94748.78
Rich						
Average value of the group (Rs)	12355.27	949.75	790.71	229.41	92.05	-
No. of households reporting	68(100.00)	59(86.76)	12(17.65)	1(0.47)	1(0.47)	2(2.94)
Average value per reported household	12345.27	1091.17	4480.69	15600.00	3130.00	-

Note: Figures in the bracket indicate percentage of total households in the group. For explanation, see text.

---

5. The household provided 50 per cent of the margin money for the purchase of a mini Truck, (1.6 ton capacity, diesel operated).

So far as the pattern of assets formation indicates the nature of surplus use, one may conclude that the absentee house-holds use their surplus for non-productive assets more than the other surplus earners do. Among productive assets, land is in fact the only asset they really care for. Seldom do they use the surplus for farm implements and allied agricultural activities. Their involvement in tertiary activities is negligible.

The Semi-Absentee: Less than one fifth of the assets of the semi-absentee is in the form of unproductive assets. This is 31.15 per cent lower than the corresponding percentage figure for the absentee. This shows that this class is relatively less inclined to unproductive expenses. However, the structure of the unproductive assets do not differ in a noteworthy way from that of the absentee.

The structure of productive assets of this class has some distinct characteristics. First, it invests about 7 per cent on farm machinery and livestock which shows that they care for asset formation in the form of farm machinery and livestock - a feature which is hardly consistent with that of traditional rentier class. Secondly, they invest 12.70 per cent of productive assets in the form of trade, commerce and other tertiary activities. As proportion of total assets of this class, this is low. In fact, as we have already noted, tertiary sector itself is not an important area of surplus use for the surveyed households.[6] However, it has been noted that about 95 per cent of total investment in tertiary sector is accounted for by this class. From this, one may infer that the semi-absentee households utilise, whatever scope there exists for productive recycling of surplus outside agriculture, particularly to tertiary sector.

About the involvement of this class in tertiary activities table 5.7 gives some information which should be noted. The incidence of involvement in different types of tertiary activities is not uniform among the households belonging to this category. While most of the semi-absentee households have reported their involvement in trade, only 48.84 per cent of the semi-absentee households have incidence of entering into agribusiness. The percentages are still lower in case of 'transport' and 'miscellaneous activities' like maintaining husking

---

6. Of course, the basis of such a comment is not that robust. In our survey, we could not estimate the financial assets; measures of inventories also suffered from serious underreporting. Due to these shortcomings, assets in tertiary sector might have been underestimated.

mill, petrol pump, etc.

So far as the pattern of surplus use is reflected through the structure of assets, one may note that the semi-absentee is tilted more to productive use of surplus than the absentee. They utilise every possible opportunity, including tertiary openings, for such investments.

The Rich Farmer : Like the semi-absentee, a typical rich farmer retains more than 80 per cent of his assets in the form of productive assets. However, most of the productive assets of this class are in agriculture. Assets in the form of lands, agricultural equipment and machinery, livestock and allied agricultural activities constitute 99.46 per cent of total productive assets of a rich farmer. Hence, unlike a semi-absentee, a rich farmer invests very little in tertiary sector (outside agriculture). In that sense his behaviour is similar to that of an absentee who keeps 99.91 per cent of productive assets in agriculture. His difference with an absentee, however, is that an absentee keeps almost all of such assets in the form of land (97.53 per cent) whereas a rich farmer retains a considerable amount (11.53 per cent) in the form of agricultural equipments and livestock.

So far as the nature of surplus use is expressed through the pattern of asset formation, one may note that the rich farmer is different from both the absentee and the semi-absentee. Unlike an absentee, the rich farmer does not use surplus in a substantial way for investment in tertiary activities. He does not however, lack enterprising attitude as the absentee does. He utilises surplus for recycling in agriculture more than the other two classes. Such an attitude is expressed through the higher percentage of assets in the form of farm machinery and livestock for this class.

Table 5.7 indicates that, all households of this class had investment in the form of farm implements. Average investments on this account was 19.55 per cent higher than that of a semi-absentee and 98.31 per cent higher than that of a reporting household in the absentee group. In allied agricultural activities, however, the difference per household was not that high. Only point to be noted is that 86.76 per cent of the rich farmers had involvement in allied agricultural activities. The relevant percentages for the absentee and the semi-absentee were 11.11 and 25.58 respectively. Allied agricultural activities are thus largely the activities of the rich farmers.

Summary and Conclusions

The analysis of asset structure lays bare some interesting aspects of asset formation in rural areas. In case of 138 households covered in the survey, there do exist three distinct patterns in the structure of assets – an important observation which could not be made from the data arranged according to the size of own land (Chapter 3).

In the first place, there exists a group of 27 households[7] whose asset structure shows the following characteristics.

a. Proportion of non-productive assets of this class is higher than those of other two classes.
b. This class has negligible involvement in trade, commerce and other tertiary activities.
c. Level of assets in the form of livestock and farm implements is poor for this class.
d. Land is the only productive asset for this class.

Coupled with the fact that direct exploitation of wage labour is poor for this class, such characteristics describe a class of exploiters who lease out a substantial part of land, earn rent income in the main, and does not recycle the surplus for technological innovation in agriculture.

43 households, termed semi-absentee, who combine exploitation through wage labour and exploitation through leasing out land[8], show following characteristics in asset formation.

a. They take up innovation in agriculture in the form of investment in farm implements on a considerable scale.
b. They utilise the openings in tertiary activities more than the other two groups.
c. Land, however, remains the main basis of exploitation for this class, too.

This class is more or less the same as the 'class of big landowners' identified in Rudra [1, Chapter 21, Section2]. As the data reveal, this is the most powerful class in terms of assets of the rural households.[9]

---

7. 25 for the major part of analysis, when the size of sample is reduced to 136. See Chapter 2.

8. See Chapter 4 for details.

9. Total asset per household of this class is 20.47 per cent and 34.21 per cent higher than those of an absentee and a rich farmer respectively (table 5.4). In terms of

It is also true that this class combines both precapitalist and capitalist forms of exploitation. However, this is not the only class of exploiters in the rural areas. According to our estimate such households constitute only 31.16 per cent of the sample households.

A substantial part of the landowners, who employ wage-labour, and participate(57 out of 68) in production, are termed as the class of rich farmers who depict the following characteristics in asset formation.

a. Land is the basis of exploitation for this class.
b. But they take up innovation in agriculture on a higher scale than the semi-absentee[10].
c. They get themselves involved in tertiary activities in a marginal way.

From the point of view of the use pattern of surplus, the following three distinct patterns, associated with three distinct classes could be identified from the patterns of asset structure discussed in this section.

a. The value of unproductive assets per household is the highest for absentee. At the indicative stage, one may, therefore, infer that absentee is the class that is the major agent for the unproductive use of surplus in the rural areas.
b. Assets per household in the form of farm implements is the highest for the rich farmers. It is thus indicated that a rich farmer is the major vehicle for productive recycling of surplus in agriculture.
c. The semi-absentee explains 95.42 per cent of investments in tertiary sector. Assets in the tertiary activities is also highest per household for this class. Thus there exists a strong indica-

---

productive assets. the asset base of this class is 26.48 per cent and 33.61 per cent higher than the absentee and the rich (table 5.4). It explains 95.42 per cent of total assets outside agriculture (prepared from table 5.5). In terms of agricultural lands and farm implements it accounts for 37.48 and 33.64 per cents of total assets respectively.

10. Assets in the form of farm implements per household is 19.67 per cent higher than that of a semi-absentee.

tion that the recycling of surplus in trade, commerce and other tertiary activities is performed chiefly by the semi-absentee

REFERENCES

1. Rudra, A. *Indian Agricultural Economics: Myths and Realities* Allied Publishers, 1982.
2. Reserve Bank Of India. *All India Rural Debt and Investment Survey;1971. Statistical Tables,* Vol. 1.
3 Reserve Bank of India, *ibid,* Vol. 2.

SIX

TEMPORAL VARIATION IN ASSET STRUCTURE AND THE MODES OF SURPLUS USE

Introduction

In the last chapter, we studied the variation in asset structure of different surplus earning classes. So far as the surplus is utilised for the formation of productive and unproductive assets of the households, such a study in terms of the cross-section data largely captures the spatial variation in the pattern of surplus use with respect to the observed households.

While the spatial study unfolds the extent or stage of development of one or the other pattern of asset configuration it excludes from the purview of its consideration the pace of such developments. This is a limitation that can be overcome only by extending the study to a dynamic analysis that considers variation of the value of the variates over time. In the analytical framework where the pattern of asset formation is largely determined by the pattern of recycling of surplus, such a study may also help one understand the nature of surplus recycling with respect to the surveyed households.

But there are problems associated with the temporal study. In spatial analysis we measured assets in terms of current prices; money served as common numeraire in terms of which the heterogeneous assets could be added up. In a time series analysis, we do not find it advisable to follow that procedure because the time series of the money value of assets would include a reasonably high inflationary component that imparts a positive bias in the growth rate. The standard procedure of applying a price index for neutralising the inflationary pressure can not be applied primarily because there does not exist any standard index (e.g., the wholesale price, agricultural commodity price, or consumer price index) for assets of the agricultural households. We ourselves could have constructed such an index on the basis of the base-year or terminal year quantities (weights) of various items of assets included in this survey. But we felt discouraged to take up such an exercise because there had been definite indications that, the relative weights of the different items of assets had changed over the decade. The variations did not follow a systematic pattern so much so that neither a Laspeyres nor a Paasche's or any other index could have escaped bias.

In an era of runaway inflation, unless one finds out a method of neutralising the inflationary factor while analysing the economics of temporal variation in assets of the households, the true variation in the rate of assets-formation would be grossly overestimated, as it has been in case of some recent studies.[1] Since we do not find a satisfactory method for neutralising the inflationary factor at aggregate level, we are constrained to abandon the idea of studying intertemporal behaviour of the combination of assets configurations. We rather decided to take up a less ambitious project of constructing such growth rates at disaggregate level, i.e., for individual items of assets measured in non-price quantitative units. Such a study discounts the inflationary bias and describes the real rate of growth for individual items of assets.

The cost of having recourse to such a quantitative analysis in terms of real rates of growth is rather high, because one fails to gather an overall information from such a disaggregate analysis. However, some indicative analyses could be performed on the basis of such data, so that one gets an overview of the aggregate situation.

---

1. Consider, for example, the compound growth rate of gross capital expenditure undertaken by cultivators calculated in Modi [1] with respect to RBI data for 1971-72 and 1961-62. It might be noted that in Modi [1, table 10] the compound growth rate for ten out of fifteen states, implicit in two end point observations was less than 8.8 per cent, the implicit compound growth rate of wholesale prices (see [2] page 91). With a reasonable assumption that the prices of capital goods in agriculture have registered a rise at least at the rate of all India wholesale prices, for 10 states, there has in fact been a *negative* growth, (i.e., decline) in gross capital formation in real terms. Such a fact is not revealed in Modi [1] which did not consider the inflationary factor and thus overestimated the growth rates.

In the following pages of the present chapter, we attempt to take up such an exercise.

There are problems associated with the measurement of real rates of growth. There are certain items in asset configuration of the households which themselves are conglomerates of some assets measured in different physical units. Consider for example, 'allied agricultural activities' which includes 'pisciculture' and 'poultry' in our case. In case of pisciculture there is long term capital cost for desilting and dewatering of ponds along with dressing and compacting of embankment; with this, there is short term circulating type capital cost involving deweeding of pond, repairing of embankments, cost of lime, manure and fertilisers. There exists dimensional incommensurability among these items so that the conglomerate called 'pisciculture' can not be measured in real terms. The same is the problem with 'poultry' whose capital cost involves cost of birds, feed and brooder which are incommensurable among one another. The measurement of 'allied agricultural activities' which is the combination of the two also becomes impossible.

Some items, however, appear in our study, as a combination and not a conglomerate of some other items of assets, each of which can be measured in real terms, but the combination of which can not be measured because of dimensional incommensurability. Consider for example, the item called 'farm implements' (agricultural equipment and machinery). In our case there are ten different types of power driven agricultural implements and equal number of different bullock driven implements and machinery for irrigation that constitute the category called 'farm implements'. One could consider the rate of growth for each of these thirty items by counting their numbers at various points of time. But no growth rate for the combination of these thirty items could be constructed because of dimensional incommensurability.

As a result, we had to be selective even when the individual growth rates were available. Though selective, the study did not exclude major items of agriculture, the focus of the present study. It examined the real rate of growth in case of agricultural land, the major income generating asset of the surveyed households. While examining the growth rate of farm implements we did not consider all the thirty items. We had been selective in this case and considered the disaggregate growth rates of seven major elements in this group, e.g., plough, bullock cart, oil engine and electric pump, shallow tubewell with pipe, tractor, tiller and thresher. Variation in income generating assets in the form of livestock was approximated by the growth rate of bullocks. The dynamic study, therefore, left an insignificant portion of income generating asset in agriculture outside its purview.

Since the productive assets in tertiary activities and unproductive assets in the form of buildings cannot be measured in real terms because they are mostly conglomerates of some assets measured in different physical units, to a large extent we could not pursue this methodology in case of tertiary and unproductive assets. For the tertiary sector, however, we performed a study on the number of persons involved in such activities. The rate of growth of such number might serve as a proxy to the inter-temporal behaviour of assets in the tertiary sector, provided that the interpersonal difference in the volume of assets in tertiary sector is not that high, which is largely true for the surveyed households.

For the unproductive assets, we have no alternative but to measure the assets in the form of buildings and household durables in monetary units. The figures for past value of such assets are very shaky, because these were derived mostly from notional estimation of the interviewers which were most often tentative in nature. These data were suspected to have a high non-sample bias. However, these were the only available data for these two attributes. For the homestead, a minor element in non-income generating assets on the other hand, we had data in non-monetary (real) units particularly for two end points (1970 and 1980). We could have calculated the compound growth rate implicit in the end point observations and avoided the inflationary bias. But in order to have comparability with other items of non-productive assets, we calculated it in monetary unit.

Thus we solved the problems related to methodology and analysed the data. The major findings are noted below.

Sale and Purchase of Land

Table 6.1 describes the distribution of sale and purchase of land during the decade (1970-1980) by size class of own land, as in 1980. More than half of the total households was involved in sales of land. They together have sold 11.89 per cent of total land of seller households. The percentage is reduced to 6.55 if we consider it as percentage of total land of all the households under consideration.

Table 6.1: Distribution of Sales and Purchases of Land by Size-Class (1970-1980).

A	B	C	D	E	F	G
5.01-7.50	4.64	50.00	9.28	0.00	0.00	0.00
7.51-10.00	10.69	75.00	14.38	0.71	25.00	2.85
10.01-12.50	25.65	100.00	25.65	11.82	66.66	17.72
12.51-15.00	11.04	47.05	23.46	8.84	29.41	30.05
15.01-17.50	3.07	21.42	14.33	1.45	35.71	4.07
17.51-20.00	6.31	50.00	14.20	0.19	6.25	3.09
20.01-22.50	9.05	64.28	13.85	0.55	7.14	7.81
22.51-25.00	5.23	55.55	9.39	0.27	11.11	2.44
25.01-27.50	6.02	57.14	10.55	1.65	28.57	5.80
27.51-30.00	6.92	50.00	13.85	0.48	25.00	1.92
30.01-32.50	4.58	55.55	8.24	2.41	22.22	10.67
32.51-35.00	17.75	75.00	23.66	2.34	12.50	0.97
35.01-37.50	11.03	100.00	11.03	0.00	0.00	0.00
37.51-40.00	2.86	33.33	8.59	5.74	66.66	17.21
40.01-42.25	0.00	0.00	0.00	0.00	0.00	0.00
45.01-47.50	4.13	100.00	4.13	1.07	50.00	2.16
55.01-57.50	0.00	0.00	0.00	0.00	0.00	0.00
57.51-60.00	0.00	0.00	0.00	0.00	0.00	0.00
65.01-67.50	8.03	100.00	8.03	0.00	0.00	0.00
70.01-72.50	0.00	0.00	0.00	0.00	0.00	0.00
97.51-100.00	2.06	50.00	4.12	0.00	0.00	0.00
115.01-117.50	2.28	100.00	2.28	0.00	0.00	0.00
Total	6.55	53.68	11.89	1.49	20.59	8.66

Notes: A : Size of land in acres (as in 1980)
B : Volume of land sold as percentage of total land of all the households in the size-class.
C : Sellers as percentage of total landowners in the size-class.
D : Volume of land sold as percentage of total land of the seller households.
E : Volume of land purchased as percentage of total land of all the households in the size-class.
F : Buyers as percentage of total landowners in the size-class.
G : Volume of land purchased as percentage of total land of buyer households.

The involvement of the households in selling operation is not uniform over classes. It varies across size-classes. In this variation, no systematic pattern is observable except for the fact that individuals in 4 (out of 22) size-classes who did not get themselves involved in selling operation belonged to very high size-classes (owned land exceeding 40 acres of land) - much higher than the limit imposed on owned land under the existing Land Reforms Act. It is also observed that the phenomenon of selling of land does not increase as we approach the ceiling limit. That the government does not encourage big holdings, does not, therefore, come as an important reason for sales of land.

One important effect of land-ceiling law might be that the big land-owners are not getting themselves involved in purchase of land in a significant way. Households with the size of individual holdings more than 55 acres are not at all found to purchase land during the last decade. For the households with the size of reported holdings around the ceiling limit, involvement in purchase of land is marginal except for only one size-class (with 37.51 to 40.00 acres of own land). Such a phenomenon should not however, be overemphasised because, the incidence of purchase of land itself is very low among the surveyed households. The amount of land purchased was only 1.49 per cent of total land of the surveyed households; only about 20 per cent of the households was involved in purchase of land .

There are 4 households belonging to a very high size-class of holdings (37.51 acres - 40.00 acres) whose behaviour pattern should be noted separately. There was one household who sold a large portion of its estate (8.59 per cent). The remaining three did not sell; they purchased land worth of 17.21 per cent of average land per family. The average description that follows from the table is that this class was involved in both sale and purchase in a big way. The real story that our master-table indicates is that the first belonged to 'absentee' who usually sold more than others and the rest were 'rich' who usually purchased more than others. Clustered in the same 'class', they depicted the average of two contradictory behaviours. Such a story thus lays bare the weakness of the analysis according to size-class of households. A description according to size-class might often depict the average of contradictory behaviours that can not be eliminated unless we change the point of reference to surplus earning classes among the surveyed households.

Sale and Purchase of Land : continued

In table 6.2 through table 6.10 we continue the discussion on asset formation of the surveyed households in the form of land, with surplus earning classes as point of reference. A detailed analysis on sales of land is done in first four tables; the phenomenon of purchase of land is analysed in next four tables. Table 6.10 describes the net situation – net of sale and purchase and analyses the pattern of asset formation in the form of land.

Table 6.2: Typewise and Zonewise Distribution of Sales of Land (in acres).

Types / Zones	Absentee	Semi-absentee	Rich	Total
Advanced	21.66(17.90) (44.53)	42.47(35.10) (51.14)	56.85(46.99) (55.12)	120.98(100.00) (51.52)
Moderate	18.65(27.01) (38.34)	29.42(42.61) (35.42)	20.98(30.38) (20.34)	69.05(100.00) (29.41)
Backward	8.33(18.60) (17.13)	11.15(24.89) (13.43)	25.31(56.51) (24.54)	44.79(100.00) (19.07)
Total	48.64(20.71) (100.00)	83.04(35.36) (100.00)	103.14(43.92) (100.00)	234.82(100.00) (100.00)

Note: Figure in parentheses denote percentages of zones (row-wise) and types (columnwise).

The households taken as a whole, sold 234.82 acres of land, which is 6.55 per cent of total land of the surveyed households. 43.92 per cent of these sales was accounted for by the rich, the relevant percentages for the absentee and the semi-absentee being 20.71 and 35.36 respectively (table 6.2). Such a description might lead one to wrong inference that the rich are more inclined to sales than the other two classes, unless one notes that the *average* sale of land per *reported* household is highest (5.40 acres) not for the rich, but for the absentee. In fact the average per reported household is the lowest for the rich (table 6.3).

Table 6.3: Zonewise and Typewise Distribution of Average Sales of Land in Acres Per Reported Household.

Types / Zones	Absentee	Semi-absentee	Rich	Total
Advanced	7.22	3.54	2.71	3.37
Moderate	4.66	4.90	3.00	4.06
Backward	4.17	1.59	2.30	2.24
Total	5.40	3.32	2.64	3.22

More than 50 per cent of total sales was reported in the advanced zone, the lowest percentage beeing reported in the backward zone.

In the advanced zone, more land for sale came from the rich. In the moderate zone, the semi-absentee and not the rich, accounted for the highest percentage of sale. In the backward zone again, the highest percentage score was that of the rich. Across zones, therefore, there had been no systematic domination of a particular class. The rich however, dominated in two out of three zones, so far as the distribution of total sales is concerned.

Considering average sale per reported household, one gets the following information. The highest per capita average sale was reported in moderate zone, followed by that in advanced and backward zones. The absentee dominated in advanced and backward zone; it was second – a close second to semi-absentee – in moderate zone. The rich never dominates. On an average, it scored third except in backward zone where it came second to the absentee (table 6.3).

73 out of 136 households[2] were involved in sales of land. 53.42 per cent of which was rich; 34.25 per cent and 12.33 per cent being the semi-absentee and the absentee. About half of the total persons belonged to advanced zones, the percentage in backward zone was 27.40, that in the moderate zone was 23.29. The rich dominated in every zone, the semi-absentee was the second, the absentee ranked a poor third (table 6.4).

Table 6.4: Typewise and Zonewise Distribution of Individuals Involved in Sales of Land

Types / Zones	Absentee	Semi-absentee	Rich	Total
Advanced	3(8.33)	12(33.33)	21(58.33)	36(100.00)
	(33.33)	(48.00)	(53.85)	(49.32)
Moderate	4(23.53)	6(35.29)	7(41.18)	17(100.00)
	(44.44)	(24.00)	(17.95)	(23.29)
Backward	2(10.00)	7(35.00)	11(55.00)	20(100.00)
	(22.22)	(28.00)	(28.21)	(27.40)
Total	9(12.33)	25(34.25)	39(53.42)	73(100.00)
	(100.00)	(100.00)	(100.00)	(100.00)

Note: Figures in the parenthesis denote percentages of zones (rowwise) and types (columnwise).

2. Out of 138 surveyed households, we had information on land in case of 136 households.

Since the entry in each cell[3] was not uniform, we normalized the information by considering the individuals involved in sales of land as percentage of total number of households in each cell (table 6.5). The table reveals that more than half of total households was involved in sale of land. 36 per cent of the absentee, 58.14 per cent of the semi-absentee and 57.35 per cent of the rich were involved in such activities. The table also indicates that 69.23 per cent of all households in the advanced zone was involved in sale of land. The relevant percentages for moderate and advanced zones were 41.46 and 46.51 respectively. From the two way classification, we also get the information that the highest percentage is for the rich in the advanced zone, the lowest is for the absentee in the backward zone. These indicate that the rich in the advanced zone is most involved and the absentee in the backward is least involved in the sales of land.

Whereas the households taken as a whole, sold 234.82 acres during the decade, they purchased only 53.47 acres of land – which is just 22.77 per cent of what they disposed of during the decade. Volume of purchase was just 1.49 per cent of total land of the households, the percentage for sales was 6.55 on the other hand. These indicate that the act of selling of land was more important than buying with respect to the big landowners.

---

3. The implication of an entry in a cell may be described in terms of the following dummy table

Type / Zone	Absentee	Semi-absentee	Rich	Total
Advanced	C_{11}	C_{21}	C_{31}	C_1
Moderate	C_{12}	C_{22}	C_{32}	C_2
Backward	C_{13}	C_{23}	C_{33}	C_3
Total	C^1	C^2	C^3	C

with $\sum_{j=1}^{3} Cij = C^i$ and $\sum_{i=1}^{3} Cij = C_j$, i = 1,2,3; j = 1,2,3

Where Cij = number of ith type of household in jth zone.

C^i = Total of a type C_j = Total of a zone:

Table 6.5: Individuals Involved in Sales of Land Distributed Typewise and Zonewise as Percentage of Total Number of Households in each Cell.

Types / Zones	Absentee	Semi-absentee	Rich	Total
Advanced	33.33	66.66	84.00	69.23
Moderate	50.00	54.54	31.82	41.46
Backward	25.00	50.00	52.38	46.51
Total	36.00	58.14	57.35	53.68

Note: See footnote 3 for explanation of entries in each cell.

This is further corroborated by the fact that the volume of land purchased per reported household was only 1.91 acres, whereas the corresponding figure for sale was 3.22 acres. The volume of land purchased was lower than the volume of land sold for each zone and for each class as the zonewise and classwise distributions of the data indicate (table 6.6 and table 6.2).

There is, however, inter-zone and inter-class variation in the purchase of land. 81.58 per cent of total purchase was accounted for by the rich. The semi-absentee accounted for 17.34 per cent. The purchase by the absentee was insignificant – it reported to have purchased only 0.58 acres of land during the decade, which comes to only 1.08 per cent of total purchase during the decade (table 6.6).

Table 6.6: Typewise and Zonewise Distribution of Purchases of Land (in Acres)

Types / Zones	Absentee	Semi-absentee	Rich	Total
Advanced	0(0.00) (0.00)	1.33(7.68) (14.35)	15.98(92.32) (36.63)	17.31(100.00) (32.37)
Moderate	0.58(2.00) (100.00)	7.23(24.88) (77.99)	21.25(73.12) (48.72)	29.06(100.00) (54.31)
Backward	0(0.00) (0.00)	0.71(10.00) (7.66)	6.39(90.00) (14.65)	7.10(100.00) (13.28)
Total	0.58(1.08) (100.00)	9.27(17.34) (100.00)	43.62(81.58) (100.00)	53.47(100.00) (100.00)

Note: Figures in the parentheses denote percentages of zones (rowwise) and types (columnwise).

More than half of total purchases was reported in the moderate zone. The advanced zone accounted for a moderately high percentage of total purchase. The performance of the backward zone was rather poor; 13.28 per cent of total purchase was reported in the backward zone (table 6.6).

The typewise and zonewise distribution of purchase of land *per reported* household (table 6.7) also confirms that the rich is the most enterprising class vis-a-vis purchase of land. On an average, a rich purchasing household has reported a purchase worth of 2.18 acres of land during the decade. This was 186.84 percent higher than that of a semi-absentee. In comparison to that of an absentee, the purchase of a rich household was 275.86 per cent higher.

Zonewise distribution of the data also indicates that the rich dominated in every zone. The semi-absentee came second. The absentee did not appear in advanced and backward zones. They purchased a very small amount in the moderate zone.

Distribution of purchase per reported household also confirms that the moderate zone dominated over other two zones. The purchase per reported households was 3.23 acres in moderate zone which is 30 per cent higher than that in advanced and more than 400 per cent higher than that in a backward zone (table 6.7).

Table 6.7: Typewise and Zonewise Distribution of Purchase of Land (in Acres) Per Reported Household)

Types Zones	Absentee	Semi-absentee	Rich	Total
Advanced	0(0.00) (0.00)	0.67	3.20	2.47
Moderate	0.58	2.41	4.25	3.23
Backward	0(0.00) (0.00)	0.36	0.64	0.59
Total	0.58	0.76	2.18	1.91

Typewise and zonewise distribution of individuals involved in purchase of land (table 6.8) shows that only 28 persons which is 20.59 per cent of total households (table 6.9) are involved in purchase of land. The comparable figure for sale being 73, this further indicates that the act of purchase is less important than sales of land. However, 20 out of 28 are from the rich; 7 belong to the semi-absentee. There is only one absentee household that was involved in purchase of land. The importance of the rich in this regard is thus reemphasised.

Table 6.8: Typewise and Zonewise Distribution of Individual Involved in Purchase of Land

Types Zones	Absentee	Semi-absentee	Rich	Total
Advanced	0(0.00) (0.00)	2(28.57) (28.57)	5(71.43) (25.00)	7(100.00) (25.00)
Moderate	1(11.11) (100.00)	3(33.33) (42.86)	5(55.55) (25.00)	9(100.00) (32.12)
Backward	0(0.00) (0.00)	2(16.67) (28.57)	10(83.33) (50.00)	12(100.00) (42.86)
Total	1(3.57) (100.00)	7(25.00) (100.00)	20(71.43) (100.00)	28(100.00) (100.00)

One interesting observation in table 6.8 is that out of 20 rich households that were involved in purchase of land, 10, i.e., 50 per cent was from the backward region. Such people constituted 47.62 per cent of total households in that region (table 6.9). Thus, 50 percent of the rich households that was involved in purchase of land was again roughly about 50 percent of the rich in the backward region. Thus, the land purchasing rich households were largely concentrated in backward region. Such households being 35.72 per cent of total purchasing households one may also conclude that the rich from the backward region is the most enterprising section vis-a-vis purchase of land.

29.41 per cent of the rich households were involved in purchase of land. The percentage for the semi-absentee and the rich had been 16.28 and 4.0 respectively. 27.27 per cent of the semi-absentee in the moderate zone had been involved in purchase of land. This is substantially higher than the comparable figures for two other zones. For the rich, as we have already noted, the concentration was in the backward zone. From the absentee, there is only one such household and this comes from the moderate zone (table 6.9).

Purchasers are mostly concentrated in the backward zone. In terms of percentage, 27.91 per cent of individuals in backward zone are involved in purchase of land. The percentage figure is 13.46 for advanced and 21.95 for the moderate zone (table 6.9).

Table 6.9: Individual Involved in Purchase of Land Distributed Typewise and Zonewise as Percentage of Total Number of Households in Each Cell

Types / Zones	Absentee	Semi-absentee	Rich	Total
Advanced	0.00	11.11	20.00	13.46
Moderate	12.5	27.27	22.72	21.95
Backward	0.00	14.29	47.62	27.91
Total	4.00	16.28	29.41	20.59

Temporal Variation in Own Land

Considering the average area of own land per household in 1970 and the amount of land sold and purchased per reported household during the decade (1970-1980), one gets the area of own land per household in 1980. The growth (decay) rate implicit in two end point observations can be calculated, so that one gets an idea about the rate of asset formation in the form of land[4] with respect to the surveyed households during the decade.

In table 6.10, we take up this exercise. It was observed that in 1970, the average area of own land for all households was 27.67 acres. The area reduced to 26.33 acres in 1980 after sale and purchase of land during the decade. This implies that, for the surveyed households, on an average, the asset in the form of land *declined* during the decade at a rate of 4.82 per cent per decade.

The rate of decline was not the same for all the surplus earning classes. The rich registered a decline at a rate of 3.74 per cent per decade; the comparable rates for the semi-absentee and the absentee had been 5.45 and 6.43 respectively. This implies that, although there had been a decline in the asset in the form of land, the rate of decline was the highest for the absentee; the lowest rate of decline was that of rich. The semi-absentee had a moderate score.

So far as the temporal behaviour of the mode of surplus use is approximated by the nature of asset formation over time table 6.10

---

4. The *effective* area of owned land should be calculated by *including* the area of land mortgaged in and *excluding* the area of land mortgaged out. But such data were not available.

indicates that during the last decade, *the big landowner of Nadia did not generally take up land as the area for recycling surplus*. This is indicated by the fact that the surveyed households didnot generally try to increase the area of owned land. This behaviour is found to be true not only for the absentee who do not usually encourage land augmenting technological progress; even the rich households who keep a substantial amount of asset in the form of farm implements, did not generally try to incur investment in the form of land.

Table 6.10: Average Area (in Acres) of Own Land Per Household and its Variation During the Decade (1970-1980)

Type Attribute	Absentee	Semi-absentee	Rich	Total
Own land in 1970	29.87	33.02	23.53	27.67
Sale per reported household	5.40	3.32	2.64	3.22
Purchase per reported household	0.58	0.76	2.18	1.91
Own land in 1980	27.95	31.22	22.65	26.33
Per cent variation	-6.43	-5.45	-3.74	-4.82

One important reason for such a behaviour pattern might be that the households under consideration being the Big Ryots according to the Land Reforms Department (i.e., households having land more than the legally permitted limit), they did not find it advisable to procure more land and invite legal complications. Another reason, cited by some of the surveyed households, was that the rate of return from agriculture was not as high as return from investments in tertiary sector or investment in financial assets (bank deposit, postal deposit, company share, etc.). So much so that they do not find it profitable to recycle the surplus to agriculture. This is a point which needs to be investigated further. However, this had not been taken up in the present study.

Land, of course, is still the major asset of the households. As we have seen in chapter 5, more than 70 per cent of rural assets is in the form of land. It is the most important productive asset of the surveyed households. A dis-investment in this sector did not, however, cause a change in the relative importance of this asset in the overall asset configuration of the households.

Other Income generating Assets in Agriculture

(a) *Traditional Farm Implements* : Out of thirty farm implements listed in the questionaire, we took up seven major implements and studied their variation over time in table 6.11. As the table indicates, there had been an overall growth in every asset during the decade. The growth rates,[5] however, differ widely. Thus, when a moderate rise (20.57 per cent) was recorded in case of plough, there had been a very high growth rate (11.00 per cent) in case of 'tractor'. Let us examine the situation in some detail.

Among the traditional implements, we have considered 'plough' and 'bullock cart'. For 138 surveyed households there had been 1.27 ploughs per household in 1970, it increased to 1.52 in 1980. Per cent variation, denoting the growth rate implicit in two end points, was 20.57. This implies that there had been gross asset formation in the form of plough at the rate of 20.57 per cent per decade.

The rate of asset formation was not the same for various classes of surplus earners. For the rich farmers, number of ploughs increased from 1.66 to 2.07 per household during the decade, thus registering a growth at the rate of 24.78 per cent per decade. In case of the semi-absentee, the growth rate was 16.66 per cent; the number of ploughs per household increased from 1.26 to 1.47. Both the growth rate and the number of ploughs in 1970 and 1980 per household were thus higher for the rich farmers.

In case of the absentee, the number of plough per household was 0.30 in 1970; it declined to 0.26. The growth rate was -12.50 per cent per decade. There was thus a decline in the number of ploughs per household. The decline was not, however, very sharp. In fact, a rearrangement of the data suggests that there was one plough per 3.85 households in 1980, whereas there has been one plough per 3.33 households in 1970 for the absentee household. However, what is clearly indicated in the data is that, true to its class nature, the absentee class did not take fresh venture for cultivation under own supervision by taking recourse to new investment in ploughs; in fact, such activities marked decline during the decade.

---

5. Growth rates were not calculated in terms of numbers per household. They were calculated by considering the total number of implements with respect to absentee, semi-absentee, rich, and total households, available in the master table.

Table 6.11 Variation in Some Selected Income Generation Assets in Agriculture (1970-1980)

	Absentee			Semi-Absentee			Rich			Total		
	I	II	III	I	II	III	I	II	III	I	II	III
Plough	0.30	0.26	-12.50	1.26	1.47	16.66	1.66	2.07	24.78	1.27	1.52	20.57
Bullock cart (regular)	0.15	0.11	-25.00	0.74	0.81	9.30	0.83	1.00	19.29	0.67	0.77	13.97
Bullocks	0.56	0.52	-06.60	2.74	3.40	23.72	3.06	4.09	33.65	2.47	3.17	28.45
Oil Engine & Electric Pump	-	-	-	0.16	0.16	0.00	0.10	0.46	342.86	0.10	0.28	171.42
Shallow Tubewell with pipe	0.11	0.18	66.66	0.16	0.77	371.42	0.32	0.90	177.27	0.23	0.72	209.38
Tractor*	-	-	-	-	0.02@	-	0.01	0.16	1000.00	0.007	0.08	1100.00
Tiller	-	-	-	-	-	-	0.01	0.03	100.00	0.007	0.01	100.00
Threasher	-	-	-	0.05	0.05	0.00	0.01	0.08	500.00	0.01	0.05	300.00

Notes: I.: Number in 1970 per household in the group
II.: Number in 1980 per household in the group
III.: Percentage change (+ve or -ve) during the decade
* For comment, see the text.
@ Introduced by one household in 1977

Percentage changes were calculated in the following way

$$\frac{\text{Total No. in 1980 - Total No. in 1970}}{\text{Total no. in 1970}} \times 100$$

The overall picture pertaining to investment in the form of plough is, therefore, that there was dis-investment in case of the absentee; the rich and the semi-absentee, on the other hand, did incur investment in plough; between the two, the rate of investment was higher for the rich. Since the rate of growth as well as the number of entries were higher for the last two clases, the combined effect for the 138 surveyed households was that there was a definite increase in the number ploughs of the households, as a result of which it registered a growth to the extent of 20.57 per cent per decade.

The condition with respect to the bullock cart (regular) was more or less the same. For the rich, it recorded a growth rate worth of 19.29 per cent per decade, the relevant rate for the semi-absentee was 3.30. In case of the absentee, it registered a decline at the rate of 6.6 per cent per decade.

(b) *Non-Traditional Farm Implements* : In case of non-traditional implements, the fact is somewhat different. It is reported that there had been no oil-engine and electric pump, tractor, thrasher or tiller for the absentee household. However, there was one shallow tubewell per 9 households in 1970; the figure rose to 5 in 1980. This gives a growth rate worth of 66.66 per cent per decade. This clearly indicates that the absentee do not incur investment in modern farm implements except moderately in case of shallow tubewell.

The semi-absentee did not have tiller. But they did have oil engine and electric pump, tractor, thrasher, and shallow tube well with pipe. The rate of growth in case of shallow tubewell was 371.42 per cent. In case of other implements, they did not achieve any growth.

The rich possessed all the major modern farm implements. In every branch they registered a high rate of growth as the ninth column of table 6.11 indicates. The conclusion that this description warrants is that the rich had recourse to investment in modern farm machinery at a fast pace. Coupled with other information this indicates that the rich had a strong motive for innovation which was shared by the semi-absentee only in a marginal way. The absentee did not have almost any motive for innovation in modern farm implements.

However, the quantitative growth rates described here exaggerates the extent of innovation in agriculture. Considering oil-engine, shallow tubewell and tractor, we find that the use of such non-traditional implements per acre of owned land was very poor, even in case of the rich farmer. The number of oil engine and electric pump per acre of owned land was merely 0.0042 in 1970 and 0.0203 in 1980 in case of the rich farmers (table 6.12); the relevant figures for the semi-absentee were even poorer.

Table 6.12: Per Cent Variation in Some Selected Non-traditional Income Generating Assets in Agriculture Per Acre of Owned Land

	Absentee		Semi-absentee		Rich		Total	
	1970	1980	1970	1980	1970	1980	1970	1980
Oil-Engine & Electric pump	--	--	0.0013	0.0147	0.0042	0.0203	0.0036	0.0106
Shallow Tube well with pipe	0.0037	0.0064	0.0048	0.0247	0.0136	0.0397	0.0083	0.0273
Tractor	--	--	0.0006	0.0006	0.0004	0.0070	0.0002	0.0030

In case of shallow tubewell, the score is better, but it is still poor in absolute terms. The observation that the growth rate recorded in case of tractor was 1100 per cent blurs the fact that use of tractor per acre was only 0.003 in 1980. The situation was somewhat better for the rich, but even then tractor per hectare of own land was only 0.007 in 1980 for these innovating households (table 6.12).

(c) *Livestock* : During the decade the number of bullocks, used as a proxy to livestock, increased from 341 to 438 in case of the surveyed households. The rate of growth was 28.45 percent per decade.

As we gather from table 6.11, the number of bullocks per family declined from 0.56 in 1970 to 0.52 per family in case of the absentee households, an observation that implies that the livestock registered a decline by 6.6 per cent over the decade for such households.

There was an increase in livestock to the extent of 23.72 per cent per decade in case of the semi-absentee households. The growth rate was 33.65 for the rich households.

The overall situation is, therefore, more or less the same as had been in case of the traditional farm implements. There was an overall growth explained fully by the investment of the semi-absentee and the rich. The absentee did not have even a pair of bullocks per family. (In fact, in 1980, there was one bullock per 1.92 family in case of the absentee). This is consistent with the non-enterprising behaviour of that class.

Involvement in Tertiary Activities

Involvement in allied agricultural activities, agri-business, transport, trade and miscellaneous activities[6] has been approximated, at an indicative level, by the number of persons involved in such activities. On the basis of this information, we have prepared the table 6.13 which describes the percentages of individuals involved in these activities in 1970 and in 1980.

26.09 per cent of total household was involved in allied agricultural activities in 1970. The percentages registered a more than 100 per cent increase during the decade. The growth rates differed among classes. For the semi-absentee, the percentage of individuals involved increased from 9.30 to 25.58; for the rich, it increased from 47.06 per cent to 86.77 per cent during the decade. There was no absentee involved in such activities in 1970; however, in 1980, 11.11 per cent of the absentee was involved in such activities. The growth rate was thus the highest (infinite) for the absentee. This fact must not be judged in isolation from the fact that the extent of involvement (i.e, percentage of members involved) was the lowest for absentee in 1980. Given that the number of absentee in the sample is low (19.5 per cent), this implies that the increase in involvement of absentee in allied agricultural activities does not make it an absentee-oriented phenomenon.

In case of agri-business again, the rate of growth of individuals involved is infinite for the absentee. The growth rate for the semi-absentee is also high; in fact it is higher than that for the rich. But the arithmetic of growth rate would lead one to conclude that the absentee is the most enterprising class in this regard, unless one notes that almost the half of the members in semi-absentee class was involved in agri-business, whereas, a very insignificant per cent (3.70) of the absentee – sample size of which is about 63 per cent of the sample size of semi-absentee – is involved in such activities.

Only 2.90 per cent of total population was involved in transport in 1970; the percentage increased to 7.92 in 1980. There was a high rate of growth in case of the semi-absentee but the growth rate was infinite in case of the absentee and the rich. This does not, however, indicate that transport is a rich peasant or absentee dominated

---

6. Involvement in husking mill, petrol pump, construction work and brick kiln.

Table 6.13: Percentage of Individual Involved in Some Selected Tertiary Activities in 1970 & 1980

Attributes Type	Allied Agri. activities		Agri. business		Transport		Trade		Miscellaneous	
	1980	1970	1980	1970	1980	1970	1980	1970	1980	1970
Absentee	11.11	0.00	3.70	0.00	3.70	0.00	--	--	--	--
Semi-absentee	25.58	9.30	48.84	6.98	20.93	9.30	83.72	69.77	13.95	9.30
Rich	86.77	47.06	17.65	4.41	1.47	0.00	2.90	2.90	--	1.47
Total	52.90	26.09	24.64	4.35	7.97	2.90	27.54	23.19	4.35	3.62

Note : Percentage is that of total number of respondents in respective classes.

sector. In 1970, there was no absentee or rich who was involved in transport activity, whereas 9.30 per cent of the semi-absentee was already with this activity at that time. In 1980, about one fifth of the semi-absentee was in the transport sector, the comparable figures for the rich and the absentee were 1.47 and 3.70 per cent respectively.

In trade and miscellaneous activities, there was no involvement of the absentee. The rich was involved in these activities in a marginal way (in fact, the involvement of the rich was nil in miscellaneous activities in 1980). The semi-absentee, on the other hand, was involved in trade in a big way. 69.77 per cent of individuals belonging to this class had involvement in trade in 1970; the percentage increased to 83.72 in 1980. This largely explains the observation that 23.19 per cent and 27.54 per cent of total households was involved in trade in 1970 and 1980 respectively.

Very small percentage of people were involved in miscellaneous activities both in 1970 and in 1980, so that the implicit growth rate was only 20.17 per cent. Whatever be the growth rate it is largely explained by the involvement of the semi-absentee in this activity.

Non Income-generating Assets

We have already stated that we had no alternative but to measure the non income-generating assets in terms of current prices. It has also been mentioned that the figures for past values are very shaky, because, except in case of the homestead, we had to depend on notional estimates which are likely to be biased.

Table 6.14 describes the average value per household of individual items of non income-generating assets in 1970 and in 1980 in terms of current prices. Except in case of durable household assets of the rich, data indicate a definite increase during the decade in case of all the non income-generating assets for all the three surplus earning classes. In terms of total value, the assets of the semi-absentee increased by 28.82 per cent decade. Those for the rich and the absentee were 13.62 per cent and 12.09 per cent per decade, respectively. Contrary to what is expected, the data indicates that the semi-absentee and not the absentee was more inclined to investment in non income-generating assets. In fact, the results indicate that even the rich invested more in this sector than the absentee – the rate of growth of non income-generating assets of the rich was slightly higher than that of the absentee.

The table reveals that in case of building and durable household assets, the rate of growth was the highest for the semi-absentee. Only in case of homestead, however, we find that the rate was the highest for the absentee.

The absentee is reported to have increased the average value of asset in the form of homestead by 61.43 per cent. This was quite impressive a figure. But then, the same class had achieved a growth rate of the order of 10.84 per cent per decade in case of buildings. The performance was poorer in case of durable household assets where it reported only a 4.68 per cent increase.

The performance of the semi-absentee was mostly a balanced one. In case of homestead, it reported an increase of assets by 52.62 per cent per decade. In case of buildings and durables, the decennial rates of growth achieved by this class were 25.36 per cent and 34.80 per cent respectively. As a result, it achieved an overall growth rate of the order of 28.82 per cent per decade.

The rich is reported to have increased assets in the form of homestead by 37.53 per cent per decade. The rate of growth was 21.04 per cent in case of buildings. But the overall growth was only 13.62 per cent, due to a negative growth rate in case of durables.

A negative growth rate of the order of 11.91 per cent per decade is rather perplexing. We do not find any reason why the durable assets should register a decline in absolute terms, particularly for the rich, during the decade. May be, there exists a bias (in the form of underreporting in 1980) in the data. This is a possibility that we do not rule out because, the data were mostly notional.

The Temporal Variation in Assets and The Nature of Surplus Recycling

The intertemporal behaviour of asset configurations of various surplus earning classes is determined by the nature of surplus recycling, because, it is through the act of surplus recycling that the asset configurations change over time. Such being the causal connection, inversely, the intertemporal behaviour of asset configurations of various surplus earning classes would describe, *inter alia*, the nature of surplus recycling of those classes, at least in an indicative way. With the help of this theoretical clue we shall attempt to trace the nature of surplus recycling of the surplus earning classes from the

Table 6.14: Typewise Distribution of Average Value (Rupee) Per Household of Indovidual Items of Non Income. Generating Assets in 1970 and in 1980 at Current Prices

Attributes / Types	Homestead 1970	Homestead 1980	Building 1970	Building 1980	Durable Household Assets 1970	Durable Household Assets 1980	Total 1970	Total 1980
Absentee	4321.25	6975.73	44525.30	49351.43	21595.00	22605.17	70432.25	78951.33
	(61.43)		(10.84)		(4.68)		(12.09)	
Semi absentee	2572.21	3935.82	42302.51	53038.04	13870.75	18697.38	58740.47	75671.24
	(52.62)		(25.36)		(34.80)		(28.82)	
Rich	1947.33	2678.21	29731.58	35990.03	10517.37	9264.95	42191.22	47937.20
	(37.53)		(21.04)		(-11.91)		(13.62)	

Note: Figures in the parenthesis denote per cent variation over the decade.
Row-wise additions may differ marginally from total, due to rounding off at various stages.

study of the intertemporal behaviour of assets that has been developed in previous sections of this chapter. We shall take up this study for three surplus earning classes separately.

Absentee: A typical absentee was not reported to recycle his surplus for increasing the area of owned land although land is virtually only productive asset of this class. He invests marginally in farm implements. His involvement in tertiary sector is poorer. He is, however, found to recycle surplus for building up non-productive assets. In fact, as we found in the previous chapter, the proportion of non-productive assets of this class is higher than those of other two classes. This is consistent with common wisdom. But then, in non-productive assets also, the rate of investment of this class is poor, which indicates that the intensity of recycling surplus to this sector might not be as high for this class as it is usually believed. This indirectly supports the hypothesis that this class is a stagnant class in the area of agriculture and other rural activities.

Semi-absentee: A typical semi-absentee also does not recycle surplus for increasing the area of owned land. But he takes up innovation in agriculture in the form of investment in farm implements, both traditional and modern, on a considerable scale. Extent of his involvement in tertiary activities has been described in the previous chapter, on the basis of which one may infer that the semi-absentee tries to utilise tertiary openings at a moderately high rate.

It has also been found that a semi-absentee does not ignore non-productive assets as areas of recycling of surplus. In fact, a semi-absentee utilises these areas more than an absentee or a rich does. Of course, this is not the major area of investment for this class.

The behaviour of asset configuration of the semi-absentee therefore, indicates that a semi-absentee utilises all possible avenues, both productive and unproductive, for recycling of surplus (except, of course, land). This implies that in case of the semi-absentee, the capitalist and pre-capitalist modes of surplus recycling co-exist, possibly in a non-contradictory way.

The Rich peasant: It is queer but true that rich peasants do not recycle surplus for increasing the area of own land. However, they do use surplus for incurring land augmenting technological progress. They invest in traditional and non-traditional farm implements more than the semi-absentee or the absentee.

The data do not permit us to hold the view that the rich do not take up tertiary activities as an area of investment. Nor does it suggest that they are averse to unproductive assets. Only thing that should be noted is that they take up agriculture as the most important area of surplus recycling. Such a distinct pattern does not emerge in case of the semi-absentee.

REFERENCES

1. Modi, A. Rural Resources Generation and Mobilisation: *Economic and Political Weekly, Annual,* 1983.
2. Choudhuri, P. *The Indian Economy*; Vikas Publishing, 1978.

SEVEN

A NOTE ON CURRENT CONSUMPTION OF NON-DURABLES BY THE HOUSEHOLDS

Introduction

It might be recalled that we proposed to examine the modes of surplus use by defining surplus as unearned income[1] and identifying the ways in which the surplus might be utilised by the households. Logically speaking, there are two ways of utilising surplus. First, the surplus might be utilised for building up durable assets which may be income generating type or otherwise. Secondly, the surplus may be utilised for current consumption of non-durables. In last two chapters, we discussed the first method of surplus utilisation by considering first the spatial and then the temporal variation of the asset configurations of the households.

In this chapter, we propose to discuss the nature of current consumption of the surveyed households. There are various types of consumption expenses incurred by the households. For example, there are expenses on food items which are either in cash or in kind. There are expenses to meet non-food needs, e.g., clothing, fuel and light, educational and medical expenses, etc. There are again expenses on (excesses in) luxury, often expressed through marriage expenses, or expenses on festivals. In the questionnaire, such items are listed in reasonable detail.

In order to study the nature of current consumption of non-durables, we decided to study the nature of expenses incurred on

1. See footnote 2, Chapter 3.

these items.

Due to paucity of time and fund, we could not, however, examine each item of current consumption. We had to economise. We therefore selected the major areas of such expenditure and examined the inter-class variation in the nature of expenditure on such items.

Thus, we considered first the expenses on food items, which largely describes the standard of living of the households. Secondly, we examined the expenses on (excesses in) luxury. The first is expected to unfold the variation, if at all, in the standard of living of the households grouped in three classes. One may get an idea about variation among the surplus earning classes with respect to unproductive and conspicuous current expenses in the form of expenses on marriages, festivals, etc., from the second study.

Standard of Living

Cereals including pulses were not usually purchased from market.[2] Salt, spices, edible oil[3] and some other items were often purchased from market. We, however, collected the data on monthly consumption of each item separately and imputed their prices to get monthly expenditure on food items, as far as practicable. In some cases, the respondents themselves furnished information in monetary terms of expenses on non-cereal consumables. We had to accept them and calculate the total monthly expenditure on food items after inputing the cost of cereals consumed.

Table 7.1 describes the expenses on food items by the households arranged in three groups, namely, absentee, semi-absentee and rich. Average expenditure on food items per family was Rs.559.85 according to this description. 62.31 per cent of such expenses was on non-cereals; the expenditure on cereals was only 37.69 per cent. This pattern is largely retained separately in case of each of the three classes. This is rather peculiar, particularly when one notes that the data on household consumer expenditure collected by the National Sample Survey, potrays quite a reverse picture.[4]

---

2. Some households reportedly purchased wheat in order to supplement the cereal requirements.

3. Reportedly purchased from market in a large number of cases, although Nadia is an oilseed producing district.

Table 7.1 Average Monthly Expenditure on Food Items by Various Types of Family (Rupees in 1980)

	Cereals	Non-cereals	Total
Absentee	222.54	358.15	580.75
	(38.32)	(61.67)	(100.00)
Semi-absentee	246.90	352.82	599.72
	(41.17)	(58.83)	(100.00)
Rich	190.00	346.06	536.86
	(35.54)	(64.46)	(100.00)
All households	211.01	348.89	599.85
	(37.69)	(62.31)	(100.00)

The reason might be that the cereal consumption was underreported systematically by all the classes, presumably due to the fact that such items did not involve cash expenditure. It is a common experience that due to poor system of household accountancy, expenses in non-monetary terms are often under reported.

Assuming that the bias is distributed uniformly among all the classes, we find that the inter-group difference with respect to consumption of food items is rather small among the surveyed households. Thus, an average absentee family consumes 3.27 per cent less than a semi-absentee. A rich farmer consumes only 11.70 per cent less of food items than a semi-absentee.

Our data do not, therefore, permit us to hold the view that an absentee maintains a better standard of living than the others. So far as the standard is described through average monthly expenditure on food items by the surveyed households, in fact, there is hardly any difference among the surplus earning classes as regards the standard of living.

Excesses in Luxury

The second major indicator through which the inter-group differences in current consumption of non durables are expressed is the

---

4. Consider for example, the NSS data on consumer expenditure on 13th round (All India : Rural) which shows that in the combined sample 59.76 per cent of total expenses on 'food total' was on 'foodgrains'. In the 16th round, the relevant percentage was 64.54. (prepared here from [1] and [2]).

'excesses in luxury'. Such items describe the unproductive and conspicuous current expenses of the households, which arrest the productive recycling of surplus. Donation, marriage, puja and such other festivals, birth ceremony, litigation, rites concerning death are the six items[5] expenses on which are included in this section. We considered only cash expenses on these items which were incurred by the households only during the year of survey. We did not consider lumpy type expenses on such non-durables which were incurred in the previous financial years. Such an exclusion was rather costly because as a result of this exclusion, we failed to examine the inter-temporal behaviour of consumption of non durables. However, such an exclusion was necessary because, the time series data on the consumption of non-durables were very shaky.

The data on average annual expenses on current consumption of non-durables in the form of excesses in luxury per household are noted in table 7.2. It shows that average expenses per household was the highest for the absentee (Rs. 32385), which is, in fact, 2.82 times higher than that of a semi-absentee. In comparison to a rich household, an absentee incurs 75.97 per cent higher consumption on (excesses in) luxury. The absentee is thus more inclined to conspicuous consumption, than other two classes.

Table 7.2 : Average Annual Expenses on (Excesses in) Luxury (Rupees in 1980).

	Percentage of Household reported	Average expenses (per household)
Absentee	58.32	32385
Semi-absentee	47.38	8477.69
Rich	21.78	18403.61

Items included: Donation, Marriage, Puja, Birth ceremony Litigation, Death rites.

Percentage of households involved in such conspicuous expenses is the highest in case of the absentee. The semi-absentee comes second. The percentage of the rich involved in such expenses is rather low – 21.78 per cent of the rich is reported to have incurred such conspicuous expenses.

The absentee being the most backward class vis-a-vis productive

---

5. These are the major items mentioned by the respondents.

recycling of surplus, it is only expected that the level of conspicuous expenses would be highest for this class. But the table also indicates that the semi-absentee, which combines pre-capitalist mode of exploitation with the capitalist one, is not the second in rank with respect to conspicuous expenses. The rich which is the most enterprising class in agriculture, is found to incur such expenses 1.17 times higher than the semi-absentee, on an average. This is explained by the fact that the semi-absentee is not a backward class with respect to productive recycling of surplus, although it does not recycle surplus in agriculture to a large extent, as the rich does.

To sum up, therefore, we may observe that the difference among surplus earning classes is not very high, so far as the current consumption of non-durables in the form of expenses on food items is concerned. The difference, however, is quite high with respect to expenditure on 'excesses in luxury', the other item of current consumption of non durables considered in this study. The absentee, which does not take up productive recycling of surplus in a big way, is found to indulge in such expenses at a higher rate than that of semi-absentee and the rich.

REFERENCES

1. S.K. Gupta and D.S. Ramaratnam. Consumer expenditure Surveys and Family budget Enquiries, *Data Base of Indian Economy*, Vol. 2, Statistical Publishing Society, Calcutta, 1975.
2. N. Bhattacharjee. Studies On Consumer Behaviour in India, *A Survey of Research in Economics*, Vol. VII, ICSSR, 1978.

EIGHT

MODE OF PRODUCTION IN NADIA AGRICULTURE

In Lieu of Introduction

A mode of production is described as a combination of the mode of surplus generation and its utilisation. Associated with a particular pattern of surplus generation, there exists a corresponding pattern of surplus utilisation. For the standard categories like the 'feudal mode of production' or the 'capitalist mode of production', this is more or less obvious. Under feudalism, where surplus is extracted from possessors of means of production (land) by exercising non-market control over direct producers, there exists a corresponding mode of surplus use which is different from that under capitalism. The feudal appropriators typically utilised the surplus for the purpose of consumption. In case of feudal lord, the surplus supported his excesses in luxury. In a distinct capitalist mode of production, where surplus is extracted through the market mechanism that enforces buying and selling of labour power, the typical method of surplus use is not consumption but re-investment with a view to expanding reproduction.

In a society where various modes of production coexist, the generation utilisation syndrome may assume some complex forms. This is particularly true in case of a semi-feudal society where there exists a dominant semi-feudal mode.[1] The generation-utilisation patterns of surplus associated with these modes are to be studied in order to

---

1. See introduction for explanation.

get the proper idea of the features of the existing modes of production. But, since there exists inter-penetration of different modes, in reality it becomes difficult to identify them.

Although it has been admitted by many[2] that a discussion on mode of production should cover the method of surplus use as well as the method of surplus extraction, there is hardly any empirical study that attempts to discuss the problem in this analytical framework. We were provoked to take up such an exercise precisely on account of this. But then, our study had been a small sample specific study confined to a small area. One can not draw a set of generalised conclusions on the basis of the findings of this survey. Again, there are analytical limitations of the study. For example we identified surplus earning classes by having recourse to what can be called 'a thumb rule' approach.[3] One could distinguish among various modes of surplus generation by this approach, at the cost of a good deal of analytical rigour.

So far as the mode of surplus utilisation is concerned, we did not tackle the problem directly, i.e., we did not try to measure surplus and consider its behaviour over time. Rather, we tried to measure the nature of surplus use by considering the current consumption of nondurables and the spatial and temporal behaviour of assets of the households. So far as the surplus is used for current consumption and asset formation, such a study might help one understand the nature of surplus use. But this study is rather indicative. Had it been possible to measure surplus directly, we could have presented a more thorough study on the nature of surplus use. This is another limitation of the present study that should be noted before we sum up the findings to describe the existing modes of production pertaining to the surveyed households, in terms of generation and utilisation patterns of surplus.

---

2. See, for example, [1],[2] and [3]. Utsa Patnaik's position [6] is rather ambivalent. She gives in to Chottopdhyay's equation of generalized commodity production with wage-labour [see 7]. At the same time, she maintains that a separate criterion based on re-investment of surplus is called for 'under the highly specific conditions of stagnation under colonial exploitation' due to which 'the destitute peasants turned labourers do not constitute free labourers as under capitalism'.

3. See Chapter 4, 'Criteria for Empirical classification' page 49.

Existing Modes of Production in Nadia

On the basis of the *a-priori* classification of households with respect to the nature of surplus extraction practiced by them, we identified three surplus earning classes in the district. First, there is a class of surplus earners who leases out a substantial part (around 75 per cent of owned land) to tenants and exploits chiefly through extraction of ground rent. We note this class as 'absentee' to highlight the fact that exploiters belonging to this class usually abstain from production in every sense – they do not even supervise production, generally they lease out land against ground rent. An absentee household is either a feudal landlord or a capitalist ground rent earner. However, the general trend being that the tenants associated with these households are 'small' in terms of both operated and owned land, and that very little technological innovations are used on the lease-hold lands, we conclude that the absolute ground rent component dominates in the pool of surplus and the predominant element in the class of 'the absentee' is the element of precapitalist landlordism.[4]

Such a type of surplus earner was not, however, predominant in the sample. Only about 20 per cent of the surveyed households belonged to this category.

31.16 per cent of the surveyed households belongs to a class which extracted surplus by leasing out a substantial part of their land to tenants and operating on the remaining part. We noted this class as 'semi-absentee'. The selection of nomenclature was influenced by the consideration of similar nature as had been taken into account in case of 'the absentee'. A semi-absentee is partly absent from production, but he operated on the other part of his land. A semi-absentee may not be a pre-capitalist exploiter as an absentee usually is. He may combine both the capitalist and precapitalist methods of exploitation and possibly no element dominates in his method of exploitation. For example, he leases out land to small tenants and maintains the relation of domination over and subjugation of the tenants, so that a high rate of rent is extracted; at the same time, he may himself lease in land from small owners and apply land augmenting technological innovations on the lease-hold land. He may employ free wage-labour as well as unfree attached labour on his

---

4. See Chapter 4 and Appendix 1 for further details.

operated holding. All these co-exist in a noncontradictory way so that no particular element possibly dominates over the other.

We call this a semi-feudal method of surplus extraction. It might be recalled[5] that in the era of Imperialism, as we noted, semi-feudalism may appear as a situation, where the feudal methods of surplus extraction co-exist with capitalist methods in a non-contradictory way. The method of exploitation pursued by the semi-absentee that we have described is consistent with this concept of surplus extraction under semi-feudalism.

Rich peasants, lease out land only marginally. They own and operate on land; in most cases, they also participate in production. In the main, they exploit labour which assume the form of wage-labour in very many cases. Given imperfect development of labour market, they also employ attached and semi-attached labourers; but the prevalent tendency of this class is to employ wage-labour; *per se*, their method of exploitation has strong resemblance with that under capitalist mode of production. Numerically speaking, this is the dominant class in the sample.

On the basis of what we discussed in Chapter 5 through Chapter 7, we may observe that these three classes have three distinct patterns of surplus use. Let us place them here in a summary form.

1. *Absentee* : From the spatial and temporal study on asset structure of the surveyed households, we found that a typical absentee was not reported to recycle his surplus for increasing the area of owned land, although land is virtually the only productive asset of this class. His involvement in tertiary sector is poor. He invests marginally in farm implements. He is, however, found to recycle surplus for building up of non-productive assets such that the proportion of non-productive assets of this class is higher than those of the other two classes.[6]

Given the non-productive orientation in the pattern of surplus use and also given that this class is not the most powerful asset-owning class in the rural areas[7], it seems that the destiny of this class is further decline and complete ruin in the long run.

---

5. See Introduction

6. This does not, however, indicated that the intensity of recycling surplus to non-productive sector is highest for this class (see Chapter 6.)

7. See Chapter 5

2. *Semi-absentee* : On the basis of assets, this class is the most powerful class in rural areas.[8] Again, a semi-absentee has more productive assets than the absentee and the rich. The spatial and temporal study reveals that a typical semi-absentee takes up innovation in agriculture in a substantial way, although he is more inclined to tertiary openings. His assets in tertiary sector is much higher than those of other two classes, so much so that the tertiary activities might be called semi-absentee oriented activities.

Again, the temporal study on asset configuration of the semi-absentee reveals that it does not concentrate only on income generating assets. A semi-absentee also invests in non-income generating assets. In fact he utilises these areas more than an absentee or a rich does although non-income generating assets is not the major area of investment for this class. In his case, however, investment in unproductive assets coexist, possibly in a non-contradictory way, with investment in productive assets. As a result, the semi-absentee is found to utilise all possible avenues, both productive and unproductive, for utilisation of surplus and thus emerges as the most powerful class in the rural areas.

Data on current consumption of non-durables reveal that the semi-absentee is least inclined to conspicuous consumption. His expenditure on food items, however, is marginally different from that of the absentee and the rich.

3. *Rich Farmers* : This class is not as powerful as the semi-absentee, because the asset base of this class is weaker than that of the semi-absentee. However, this class is inclined to productive recycling of surplus, as the semi-absentee is. The nature of recycling of surplus pursued by this class is somewhat different from that of the semi-absentee. A rich farmer takes up innovation in agriculture on a higher scale than the semi-absentee. But unlike the semi-absentee, his involvement in tertiary sector is marginal.

A rich farmer does not maintain a better standard of living than the absentee or the semi-absentee. He does not indulge in feudal excesses as an absentee does.

This class is weak. But there is no evidence that this class is a decaying class.

Since a mode of production is described as a combination of the

---

8. See footnote 9, Chapter 5.

mode of surplus generation and its utilisation, from the foregoing discussion, we could identify three distinct modes of production. We described them in the form of the following three summary tables :

	Mode of Surplus generation	Mode of Surplus use	Mode of Production	Comment
A.	Rack renting through domination over and subjugation of small peasants	Surplus recycled for building up non-productive assets; surplus used for conspicious consumption.	Feudal Mode of production	A decaying mode
B.	Rack renting through domination over and subjugation of small peasants, employment of free wage-labour and unfree attached labour on operated land.	Surplus recycled for building up of both productive and unproductive assets; recycles substantially to agricuture but more inclined to tertiary sector; least inclined to conspicuous consumption.	Semi-feudal mode of production	(i) Precapitalist and capitalist mode of surplus generation co exist in a non-contradictory-way. (ii) Precapitalist and capitalist mode of surplus recycling coexist in a non-contradictory way. (iii) Most powerful mode in rural Nadia.
C.	Exploitation through employment of wage-labour, also employs attached labour.	Mostly inclined to productive recycling of surplus; agriculture and not tertiary sector is the major area of surplus recycling; not inclined to conspicuous consumption.	Capitalist mode of production.	Weak but a developing mode.

Concluding Remarks

The term'semi-feudalism' is often used to describe a transitional situation where there is obvious and marked decline of feudal natural economy along with a more or less retention of feudal forms of exploitation. The logical destiny of such a society is capitalism.

The process of development of capitalism in such a society is that the feudal property is transformed into such economic forms that correspond to the requirements of capitalist mode of production; labour then comes to the formal subsumption of capital. Capital revolutionises the techniques of production, so that, subsequently there appears real subsumption of labour. the society is then transformed into a capitalist society [4, p. 1024].

The role of productive recycling of surplus in the context of transition to capitalism should be adequately emphasized. The real subsumption of labour that notes the transition, appears as the result of the capitalist act of revolutionising the technology[9] which again is the outcome of productive recycling of surplus.

Again, as pointed out by Marx, the development from formal to real subsumption is not automatic. There exists the necessity of a minimum amount of capital for the real subsumption of labour under capital to come about [4, p. 1027,1035]. This, in its turn, implies the necessity of a productive recycling of surplus at a critical minimum level, so that the transition is attained. As might be well known, such a necessary condition was satisfied by those countries where the transition was completed before the era of imperialism, when capitalism had relentlessly pursued the policy of promoting technological progress.

There is a school of thought according to which, such a transition might be thwarted in the backward countries in the era of imperialism. The economic foundation of imperialism being monopoly, 'it generates the possibility of deliberately retarding technological progress' [5, p. 276]. In such a situation, the colonies and other dependent regions which bear the major brunt of such technological retardation, might experience a situation when the transition from formal to real subsumption of labour is not automatically guaranteed. Such a situation arises because there develops the possibility of a dwarfed development of the capitalist act of revolutionising the technology in those regions, particularly in the agriculture of those countries. In other words, the productive recycling of surplus in agriculture might not attain the critical minimum level so that the transition from formal to real subsumption is attained automatically.

---

9. The causal correspondence between real subsumption and revolutionisation of technology might be expressed in the following way: the search for a constant increase in surplus value production implies a search for constant reduction in necessary labour which is attained by continuous expansion of technology when lengthening of working hour is not possible. Thus, the increase in relative surplus value is caused by the revolutionisation of technology.

The dominant mode of production in such a situation is the semi-feudal mode of production. The exploiters under this mode of production, who account for the bulk of surplus, take up a method of surplus recycling, which thwarts the development of real subsumption of labour to capital in agriculture. They siphon off a substantial part of agricultural surplus to tertiary sector so that the productive investment in agriculture does not attain the critical minimum required for transition from formal to real subsumption of labour. The reason for such a preference for investment in tertiary sector might be that the rate of return is higher in tertiary activities.

However, the growth of tertiary activities is again a function of growth of production activities in secondary and primary sector. The sluggish growth in primary and secondary sectors sets limits to tertiary activities[10] This, in turn, limits the possibility of surplus recycling in tertiary sector That such a limit has already been set in the District is revealed in the census data pertaining to trend and structure of employment in the district (see Appendix II). The sluggish growth of tertiary sector arresting the possibility of recycling of surplus at a high rate is one of the reasons that the semi-feudal exploiters take up other less profitable areas as well, for reinvestment of their surplus.

REFERENCES

1. Banaji, J. India and Colonial Mode of Production, Comment, *Economic and Political Weekly*, December, 1975.
2. Gupta, D. Formal and Real Subsumption of Labour Under Capital, *Economic and Political Weekly*, September, 1980.
3. Sau, R. On the Essence of Manifestation of Capitalism in Indian Agriculture, *Economic Political Weekly*, September, 1979.
4. Marx, K. *Capital*, Vol.1, Penguin, 1979.
5. Lenin, V. I. *Collected Works*, Vol.22, Progress Publisher, 1974.
6. Patnaik, U. On the Mode of Production in Indian Agriculture - A Reply, *Economic and Political Weekly*, September 1972.
7. Chattopadhyay, P. Mode of Production in Indian Agriculture: A preliminary note, *Economic and Political Weekly*, March 1972.

10. See appendix 2.

APPENDIX I

TENANCY, CREDIT AND AGRARIAN BACKWARDNESS

Introduction : The Selection of Tenant Households

With respect to the big landowners of our sample, the institution of tenancy was found to retain much importance. Thus, 89 out of 138 landowners reported their involvements in tenurial practices. Again, the overwhelming majority of them (73 out of 89) entered into land lease arrangements as lessors of land. Big landowners in Nadia, in our sample, thus enter into the land lease arrangements mainly as lessors of land.

Regarding the selection of tenant households we proposed to adopt the following method. For every lessor household, it was decided that an exhaustive list of the associated tenant households would be prepared. Then, for every lessor, a purposive selection would be done of not more than three tenant households – preferably one from each of landless, marginal (with the size of owned holding not exceeding one hectare), small (with the size of owned holding between one and two hectares) and medium to rich (with the size of owned holding exceeding two hectares) group of tenants.

However, this procedure could not always be observed. The terrain of our enquiry was largely inhospitable in nature. A direct enquiry to the landlord or to the tentant with the knowledge of the landlord, about tenurial practices often resulted in a very hostile or conspicuously cold response. So much so that, of the 138 landowners we could meet a section of tenants associated with only 47 households whereas we knew from people not immediately connected with the process that there were as many as 73 such lessor households. Clearly, landlord tenant interaction was of a nature that necessitated a shield from public exposure – a point which we discuss at greater length in sectionIII.

While preparing the list and surveying the tenant households, we therefore, had to bypass the landlord as far as practicable. In most of the cases, we faced a situation that forced us to labourously seek and search people not directly connected with the landlord. With the help of such people, we contacted the tenants directly and canvassed the tenant questionnaire.

The cost of such a roundabout method was that the proposed method of selecting the tenant households could hardly be observed. Approachability and reliability became the most important criteria for selecting elements of the sample households of tenants.

There is thus a two level purposiveness in the data. First, the landowners were selected with an element of purposiveness. Secondly, no systematic pattern was observed for selecting the tenant households. From statistical point of view, no generalisation can therefore be made from the sample. The result given in the next section is thus only a case study covering 85 tenant households and 47 landowner households belonging to the Nadia District of West Bengal.

I

The Landowner

Table A1 describes the size distribution of land owned by the reported lessor households. There are 73 reported households, reported in the sense that these households were reported to enter in the lease arrangement as lessors of land. No information on the size of owned land could be obtained for two households. Table A1 therefore describe the size distribution of holdings for 71 households. The data on ownership holdings were obtained either from the Land Records Department of the Government of West Bengal or from local reliable sources. In very few cases, the landowner himself disclosed any information on the size of owned land that could be relied upon.

Table A1 : Size Distribution of Owned Holding for 71[(a)] Reported Lessor Households

Size of owned land (Hectare)	Number of lessors	Absentee	Semi Absentee	Rich
4-4.99	3	0	1	2
5-9.99	35	10	20	5
10-14.99	23	6	14	3
15-19.99	4	2	2	0
20 and above	6	2	3	1
Total	71	20	40	11

(a) There are 73 lessor households, but the position of owned land could not be ascertained for 2 cases.

These households could largely be termed as big landowners with respect to the selected district. According to the Agricultural Census (1970), Nadia is a district where the middle peasants dominate. About 80 percent of the holdings in Nadia are below 2 hectares and they together represent about 45 percent of the area under cultivation, while on the other hand, only about 6 percent of the holdings have land above 4 hectares constituting about 23 percent of the cultivated area. In fact, the number of holdings above 10 hectares is very small in the district : 0.7 percent of the holdings in Nadia are above 10 hectares and this represents only 0.82 percent of the area under cultivation.

The households that were reported to practice leasing out land thus belong to the group of upper 6 percent of the landed households of the district. Again, 33 out of 71 reported households belong to the group of upper 0.7 percent of the holdings. Considering the landowners whose tenant households were included in the sample, it is found that about 50 percent of these households belong to the group of upper 0.7 percent of the holdings of the district. The rest belongs to 4 to 10 hectares group, i.e., the group which represents the upper 5.3 percent of the holdings of the district (Table A3). It could therefore be stated that the tenant households included in the sample were tied to the relatively bigger landowning households of the district.

With respect to the involvement of households in tenurial practices, the households have been divided in three broad categories. There were 20 households, reported to lease out roughly more than

75 per cent of their lands, thus earning mainly ground rent from their holdings. They have been termed 'absentee' households – absentee in the sense that they were mainly absent from the production process.

A sizeable section of the landowners were reported to lease out nearly half of their owned land and operate on the rest using both family labour and outside labour. In the absence of a better nomenclature, we termed them 'semi-absentee' households. This is the prevalent type of landowners in the sample – 40 out of 71 belong to this category.

As we have already stated, we could meet only a section of tenants associated with 47 out of these 73 lessor households. Then again, no systematic pattern could be maintained in selecting the landowner households. 15 of these households were 'absentee', only 3 were 'rich' and 27 were 'semi-absentee'. There were two households that could not be classified in this manner, because the relevant information was not available (Table A3).

The Tenant

We could trace 569 tenants associated with the 47 lessor households. The number of tenant households visited was quite small, 85 or about 15 percent of the total. The classwise break up, given in table A2, shows that about 15 and 12 percent of the tenants associated with the semi-absentee and absentee households respectively, have been covered in the survey. We covered about 90 percent of the tenants associated with the rich households.

No statistically regular process was observed for selecting the sample households. We can not therefore ascertain whether the selected 85 tenant households could statistically represent the bahaviour of 569 tenants, or whether the classwise break up of tenants has any representativeness with respect to the population.

About the other character of the sample, we note that about 34 percent of the selected tenants were tied to the absentee households; more than 55 percent maintained tenurial contracts with the semi-absentee households. The rest, quite a negligible percentage, was tied to the rich peasant households. We, therefore, conclude that the selected tenant households were mainly connected with the absentee and the semi-absentee landowning families.

TABLE A2: Description of Tenant Households and their Association with Various Types of Lessor Households

Types of lessor households	No. of lessor households	No. of tenants reported	No. of tenants visited
Absentee	15	242	29
Semi absentee	27	320	47
Rich	3	7	6
Could not be ascertained	2	Not available	3
Total	47	5690	85

Note: No reliable information on the number of tenants associated with two lessor households could be obtained. However, three tenants associated with these households could be visited.

The Bargaining Position of Lessor vis-a-vis Lessee

The most important economic factor that shapes bargaining position regarding terms and conditions of tenurial arrangement is the asset position of the lessor and the lessee. Land under ownership right being the most important asset of the rural households, the position of the sample households as regards the size of owned land might give some idea about the bargaining position of the tenants vis-a-vis their landlords[1].

The latest NSS findings indicate that in West Bengal the lessor is not always more resourceful than the lessee. More than 70 percent of the lessor households, according to the NSS, are small and marginal farmers; they account for about 53 percent of the area leased out. More than 70 percent of the lessee households are again small and marginal farmers (on the basis of owned land) accounting for more than 75 percent of the area leased in[2].

It is no wonder that the typical lessor that we visited does not confirm the NSS finding because we chose big landowners as the point of reference. The size distribution of owned land for the sample of 47 (excluding two for which no information on owned land could be obtained) landowners shows that with respect to the size of

1. The bargaining position also depends on various social, political and cultural factors of the rural societies. These could not, however, be covered in this survey.

2. National sample survey, 26th round; Report No. 215, pp 67-68.

owned land all the lessor households belong to the 'above 4 hectares' or the highest NSS size-class. We have even such households as have more than 20 hectares land under ownership right. Further details are given in table A3. We need not elaborate it here.

Table A3 : Size Distribution of Owned Holding for 45* Lessor Households

Sizeclass of owned land (Hectare)	No. of lessors	Absentee	Semi absentee	Rich
4-4.99	2	0	1	1
5-9.99	21	7	14	0
10-14.99	14	5	7	2
15-19.99	4	2	2	0
20 and above	4	1	3	0
Total	45	15	27	3

* No information on owned holding for 2 lessors.

The typical lessee household in the sample is, however, a small and marginal farmer, in the sense that the size of his owned land does not exceed 2 hectares. About 75 percent of the tenants belong to this category. 20 percent of the tenant households had not land under ownership holding. 'Medium to rich' farmers (loosely defined as farmers with the size of owned land exceeding 2 hectares constitute a conspicuously low percentage. Thus, the sample of tenant households visited by us is largely dominated by the landless, marginal and small farmers (Table A4).

Since the bargaining power of the tenant is positively related to the size of the ownership holdings of the tenant, the significance of the predominance of the landless, small and marginal farmers in the sample of tenant households can easily be appreciated. These tenants generally have poor bargaining power vis-a-vis their lessors who have definite leverage owing to their superior asset base. As a result, there develop various patterns of domination and exploitation, which cannot be properly analysed in terms of market relations only.

TABLE A4 : Sizeclass Distribution of Operational Holding & Ownership Holding of 85 Tenant Households

Size of ownership holding (hectare)	Size of operational holding (hectare) 0.1-0.99	1-1.99	2 & above	Total
0	12	1	4	17
0.1 - 0.99	18	19	10	47
1 - 1.99	-	12	5	17
2 and Above	-	-	4	4
Total	30	32	23	85

II

Pattern of Tenure

The pattern of tenurial arrangements considered in this section pertains to the major crops produced on the leasehold land. Most of such holdings reported a monocrop pattern namely the cultivation of early Kharif paddy(Aus) or jute on highlands and Kharif paddy(Aman) on low lands. Only 18 our of 82 cases reported double cropping on the leased land. This implied the adoption of a HYV crop (Boro, a summer paddy) in addition to one of the kharif crops. It is interesting to note that we did not encounter a single case where wheat cultivation had been adopted in the leasehold land, although Nadia is a major wheat producing district of West Bengal.

A cropwise breakup of information on tenancy would therefore, cover 100 cases. However, the results given below are those of only 82 cases. We consider only the advance crop (Boro) for the 18 households reporting two crops a year. We did not find it necessary to include information pertaining to traditional crops for these 18 households because they hardly differ from those of the remaining 64 cases.

The Tenurial Arrangement : Crop Share

In the overwhelming majority of the cases, sharecropping is the principal form of tenancy. Out of 79 cases, only 10 reported fixed rent tenancy. The rest, a little less than 84 percent of the total cases, were under share-cropping arrangements (Table A5). This observation is consistent with the NSS finding, regarding the forms of tenurial arrangements in West Bengal. The large scale survey of Bardhan and Rudra (1980) and the pilot survey of Rudra (1975a) also revealed more or less the same pattern. From these we conclude that there is nothing peculiar with respect to tenancy arrangements for the selected households in Nadia. As in other parts of West Bengal, here also, share-cropping is the principal form or tenancy.

Table A5 : Association Between Crop Share and cost Share
Lessee : Lessor

Crop Share	Cost Share A	B	C	D	E	Total
75 : 25	-	-	-	3(2)	-	3(2)
66.7 : 33.3	1	-	-	8(3)	-	9(3)
62 : 38	-	-	-	3(1)	-	3(1)
50 :50	26(6)	3(3)	2	19	-	50(9)
Fixed Amount (crop)	1(1)	-	-	2	-	3(1)
Fixed Amount (cash)	-	-	-	6(2)	1	7(2)
No crop share	-	-	-	4	-	4
No information	-	-	-	3	-	3
Total	28(7)	3(3)	2	48(8)	1	82(18)

Notes (i) A = 50 : 50 of total material cost
B = Total of seed and fertiliser by one and water by the other.
C = Total material cost (0: 100)
D = No cost share (100 : 0)
E - No information

(ii) There are 4 cases where neither the crop nor the cost is shared. This resulted from dispute regarding tenancy contract.

(iii) Figure in the brackets indicate the adoption if the HYV crops (Boro - a summer paddy)

(iv) By 'Material cost' we imply the cost of seed. fertiliser. manure. pesticides and water.

The crop sharing arrangement, however, assumes only 4 different forms, the proportion of share clustering around a simple rational fraction. Compared to the corresponding findings of the survey of Bardhan and Rudra (1980) covering 110 villages spread all over the state which reported as many as 11 different types of share proportions for West Bengal, our data reveal a relatively simple picture. In a situation with improper development of the lease market, the observed variations in the patterns of crop sharing arrangements seem to correspond largely with the spatial spread of the number of observations - a feature which could not adequately be captured by the present survey due to its small district specificity.

Table A5(a) : Measure of Association

	Attributes	Value of contingency x^2	Degree of freedom	Comment
1.	The adoption of the HYV crops and the tenant's share of the crop	3.146	1	Not significant at 5% level.
2.	Lessor's crop share and the existence of cost share	14.13	1	Significant at 1% level.
3.	Lessor's participation in cost and the adoption of the HYV crops	2.104	1	Not significant at 5% level.
4.	Lessor's participation in both cost and the decision making process of farm	12.79	1	Significant at 1% level.

There exists a marked resilience of the crop sharing arrangement on a 50:50 division of the produce. 50 out of 65 cases of share tenancy reported a 50 percent share of the crops for the tenant. Other arrangements account for a low percentage of the total. Thus a 75:25 share proportion between the lessee and the lessor has been observed only in 3 cases. Another 9 cases reported the share arrangement of 66.7:33.3. A 62:38 share ratio between the lessee and the lessor was observed in another 3 cases. All these account for only about 23 percent of the total cases under share cropping. In this context, it should also be noted that we did not encounter a single case where the tenant's share was less than 50 per cent of the produce.

Share cropping is the principal form of tenancy in case of HYV crops, too. Only 3 out of 18 cases involving the HYV crops were under fixed rent tenancy, leaving as many as 15 cases under sharecropping arrangements. Although the majority of such crop sharing cases reported a 50:50 division of the produce, it has been observed that the alternative arrangements. assuring a higher share of the produce for the tenants, have also made some advancements. Thus,

6 out of 15 cases reported more than 50 per cent share for the tenants. However, such developments do not warrant the conclusion that the land augmenting technological progress expressed through the adoption of the HYV crops generally assures a higher share for the tenant, because the measure of association between a higher share of the produce and the adoption of the HYV crops is not found to be statistically significant even at the 5 percent level (Table A5a).

The Tenurial Arrangement : Cost Share

The traditional cost sharing arrangement in West Bengal is that the landlord provides land tax and irrigation taxes, if any, and the tenant provides bullock and plough. About other input costs viz., costs of seed, manure, fertiliser and pesticides particularly in case of the HYV crops, human labour for weeding and harvesting (particularly in case of jute cultivation) and lastly the irrigation cost (cost of purchasing water from deep or shallow tubewell) if required, a wide variation in arrangement exists. The variation exists both within and among villages and among the parties concerned.

With respect to the households visited by us, it was found that the employment of human labour had always remained the responsibility of the tenants; landlords never shared it. The sharing of costs, if any, was confined to the costs of material inputs viz., seed, manure, fertiliser, pesticides and water only. The columns of table 5 describing cost sharing therefore pertain to such costs only. Again, the use of chemical fertilisers and water, the two items where the cash requirements were relatively high, was confined to the HYV crops only. The production of traditional crops, did not normally involve the use of such items, thus keeping the cash requirement for sharing the cost of material inputs in such cases relatively low.

There are 28 cases where the total material costs are shared in 50:50 proportion. Out of these, there are 7 cases of HYV crops where the cost of fertiliser, seed, water and pesticides were shared at 50 per cent basis. Regarding the HYV crops, there exists another pattern of cost share where the total amount of seed and fertiliser is supplied by one party (usually the tenant) and the charge for using water from the government deep tubewells is borne by the other (usually the landlord). Such a pattern becomes viable because, at the existing prices, this boils down to a proposition of sharing the cost at almost a 50:50 basis in terms of money.

We observed only two cases where all the material inputs were provided by the landlord. But no such case involved the production of HYV crops. On the other hand, there are 48 cases including 8 cases of HYV crops where the landlords did not participate in the cost.

Crop Share and Cost Share

The traditional pattern of crop and cost sharing in West Bengal is that the landlord gets one half of the produce without participating in the material cost of production. As our sample indicated, such an arrangement is certainly not the most dominant one, not to speak of being the only one. Thus out of 78 cases giving information on the patterns of sharing both cost and crop, such an arrangement was reported only in 19 cases, thus leaving more then three fourths of the total cases under alternative arrangements. It is interesting to note that not a single case of the adopting of HYV crops was under the traditional arrangement.

A'no cost share' arrangement is associated with the higher share of crop for the tenants in as many as 14 cases. Another 8 such cases were under fixed rent arrangements. Of these 22 cases, there are 8 cases of HYV crops. Thus, there exist 14 cases of traditional crops where the traditional arrangement has been flouted.

A 50 per cent share of the crop is more often associated with cost participation by the landlord even in case of the traditional crops. Thus, out of 41 cases of traditional crops where the landlord's share was 50 per cent of the produce, there are 22 cases where the cost participation was reported.

There is a clear indication that in case of the adoption of the HYV crops a 50 percent sharing o the crop warranted a cost participation on a 50 per cent basis. The cases of no cost share, on the other had, were invariably associated with higher share of crop for the tenants.

Is there any significant association between the landlord's crop shares and the existence of cost shares? The above description fails to give a precise answer. We therefore computed a contingency x^2 value that measured the extent of association in formal terms. It was found that the association is statistically significant even at 1 percent level of significance. (Table A5a)

III

Interlocking of Market and Now-market Forces

Table 5 indicates that there exists a multiplicity in crop and cost sharing arrangements with respect to the landowners and tenants appearing in the sample. In neo-classical economics, preoccupied with the efficiency of resource allocation in terms of factor prices, such a phenomenon could be explained either in terms of varying bargaining power of individual lessors and lessees or in terms of differential risk aversion behaviour of the parties in the general setting of free decision making process under competitive market conditions[3]. In some cases, farm size used as a screening device appears as an explanatory factor.

The fundamental weakness of such an approach is that it is based on 'methodological individualism' according to which the economic interaction among the individuals is assumed to be sustained through the universal functioning of price mechanism. Obviously, the universal existence of markets (more often, the competitive markets) without which the price mechanism cannot operate is the prerequisite for functioning of any model based on such a methodology. The limitation of such an approach becomes apparent when one enters into such areas where non-price or non-market forces are present. Agriculture of backward countries is one such area. The conventional economic analysis still tries to consider these economies in terms of market forces by restricting the assumptions of the models developed in the context of competitive markets. The poverty of such analyses have been pointed out by other critics[4]. Instead of repeating them, in this section we shall submit some evidences in support of the contention that the non-market forces are strongly present in the rural areas of a backward country like India. These non-market forces, interlocked with some market forces give rise to such a situation where the traditional tools of the neo-classical economics, developed in the context of studying the market economies, lose

---

3. Bell, C & Zusman, P(1976), Stiglitz, J.E.(1974) and Newberry, D.M.G.(1977).

4. For example, Bharadwaj, K. (1980), Lecture 2 and Lecture 3. Also, Godelier, M(1972) and Green, F & Nore, P.(ed.), (1977). In this section, we follow the approach of Bharadwaj (1980).

much of its relevance.

The Semi-Feudal Authority

The tenants in West Bengal, popularly known as 'Bargadars' were largely tenants-at-will; in most cases they had no occupancy right over the soil. The landowners, known as 'Jotedars' could evict them at any time with impunity from lawenforcing authorities. Again, the terms and conditions regarding crop and cost shares were largely oral in nature. Mutual trust being the only basis of implementation of the contract, in case of a violation of the terms of contract, any judicial relief could seldom be obtained by the adversely affected party. People with weaker bargaining power are bound to lose in such a situation as the poor tenants often do. The crisis is further aggravated by the inadequate development of peasants' movements as a result of which the collective bargaining power of the poor tenants remains at a low level. The secular rise in population with a stagnant or declining area of land under tenancy works as an additional factor favouring the landowners who, under such conditions, find it easy to manipulate the shares in their favour. The arrangement assumes a form of 'personal contract' the terms of which are such that even the state-sponsored crop sharing ratios[5] are often flouted. Thus, in case of the tenant households visited by us, only 3 out of 79 tenants reported to have received the legally stipulated share of the produce. (These 3 tenants received 75 per cent of the produce while they themselves incurred all the productive expenses). Not a single tenant expect these three could acquire the legally stipulated share[6].

There are administrative lapses in implementing the legal provisions. But the very fact that such an illegal arrangement adversely affecting the tenants could perpetuate in this way also indicates that

---

5. The Article 16 of West Bengal Land Reforms Act states: the produce of any land cultivated by a bargadar shall be divided as between the bargadar and the person whose land he cultivates: (a) in the proportion of 50:50 where plough, cattle, manure and seeds necessary for cultivation are supplied by the person owning the land (b) in the proportion of 75:25. in all other cases'. (Source : The Land Reforms Act, 1955 with amendments up to 1980).

6. No case of landowner's participation in cost under 50:50 sharing of the crop reported provision of plough and cattle to the tenant. Even 2 cases of supplying total material costs excluded such items. Hence, all the crop-sharing arrangements reported here violated the legal recommendations.

the social power wielded by the big landowners is so strong that it could even frustrate the legislative measures, the most important elements that form the rules of civil society. Such a power emerging out of various economic and extra economic advantages enjoyed by the big landowners in the social milieu of the rural areas, could be called the semi-feudal authority of this class.

The landowners who have recourse to illegal practices by virtue of their semi-feudal authority over the tenants are always suspicious about the purpose of queries of the outsiders on the terms and conditions of tenurial arrangements. It is often thought that these queries might result in interference from outside and, as a consequence, the command they enjoy over their tenants might be disturbed. This is the primary reason for the big landowners' resistance in the form of hostilities or conspicuously cold response to the investigator's question. They simply deny the existence of such tenurial practices in their holdings. Again, with the help of their authority, they prevail on their tenants in such a way that they are also discouraged from responding effectively to investigators' questions - a problem we mentioned in section I.

'Operation Barga' and the Semi-Feudal authority

It is often stated that the Bargadars could not be protected from illegal extortion by the Jotedars because the share-cropping arrangement is often oral in nature which has no legal validity. The prerequisite for availing of legal assistance in case of deprivation from the legally stipulated share is that the tenants record their names with the Land Records Department. In fact, as the law stands now, any tenant who is deprived of his legal share of the produce is to get quick relief provided he records his name in good time. Also, a recorded tenant cannot be evicted from the land.

The Land Records Department had not taken this recording business seriously, until the Left Front government took up a crash programme in 1978 on this issue. This programme, known as 'Operation Barga' made it imperative for the Land Records Department to take initiative for recording the names of the tenants by opening special camps in the rural areas. The bureaucratic processes were also simplified.

These measures, designed to curb the semi-feudal authority of the Jotedars did not produce satisfactory results mainly because the participation of the tenants in Operation Barga was not very high. Thus, the crash programme could record the names of about 10 lakhs of tenants[7], whereas the estimated number of tenants in West Bengal is more than 20 lakhs. The big landlord specific tenant households of Nadia, visited by us, recorded even a poorer performance with respect to 'Operation Barga'. It was observed that about 73 percent of the tenants included in the sample, did not officially record their rights as tenants, they preferred to remain non-legalised share-croppers. Contrary to normal expectation, it was found that most of such farmers were landless, marginal or small on the basis of owned land, thus running the higher risk of getting evicted and receiving lower share compared to the people with higher asset base, who thus required less protection from the law enforcing authority.

There were two explicitly stated reasons for such a poor participation of the tenants in 'Operation Barga'. 16 tenants, 10 of whom are landless stated that they feared eviction, had they tried to record their rights. 'Faith in mutual relation', a non-price person-specific consideration, was the reason submitted by 20 tenants. A sizeable section of tenants, 25 out of 62, refused to answer this apparently innocent question. It is our impression that these tenants, mostly landless and marginal farmers, refused to discuss this question out of the apprehension, that this discussion might be communicated to their landlords and this might produce adverse consequences (Table A6).

Table A6 : Progress of 'Operation Barga'

	Total	Number of tenants No participating in Operation Barga	Reasons for non participation			
			Fear of eviction	Faith in mutual relations	Refused comment	Could not be ascer-tained
Landless	17	15	10	2	3	0
Marginal	47	35	5	11	18	1
Small	17	10	1	5	4	0
Rich	4	2	0	2	0	0
Total	85	62	16	20	25	1

7. Economic Times, Calcutta, March 17, 1981.

These results give some idea about the strength of the semi-feudal authority of the big landowners included in our sample. These landowners have sufficient power to keep tenancy at non-legalised levels. As a direct consequence of this, the large majority of the tenants could be deprived of the legally stipulated share of the produce. That such a move could succeed, in spite of the legislative desires and administrative directions to the contrary, indicates that the decision-making process of the tenants, under such a situation, is largely constrained and controlled by the semi-feudal authority of the landowners. Under such conditions, it seems that an analysis of multiplicity of crop and cost sharing arrangements, in terms of varying bargaining power of the individual lessor and lessee or in terms of differential risk aversion under the general setting of *free decision making process*, is completely banal. An alternative analysis, mainly socio-political in nature, that discusses the process of interaction between the semi-feudal authority and the rural masses, might give a better insight into the problem.

IV

Cost Participation and Semi-feudalism

Bardhan and Rudra (1980), Rudra (1975a), Parthasarathi (1975) and C.H.H. Rao (1975) have observed that cost sharing arrangement as a part of tenancy contracts has become prevalent in rural India. Our data do not contradict such an observation. Out of 81 cases, we find that there was participation in cost by the landlords in an many as 33 cases. Out of 65 cases of share tenancy, we find that there are as many as 32 cases, including 9 cases of HYV crops, where the landlords participated in the cost.

While considering the economic significance of landlord's participation in costs, one should note that the income of the cost participating landlord does not assume the form of pure rent, because he does not claim his share exclusively on the basis of his property rights; his claim is also based on sharing a portion of working capital supplied by him. About a century ago, Marx noted this 'as a transitory form from the original form of rent to capitalist rent[8] effected

8. Karl Marx, 'Capital', Vol 3, pp 783

through a 'metayage' or sharecropping system under which 'the manager (farmer) furnished labour (his own or another's) and also a portion of working capital (e.g., cattle) and the product is divided between tenant and landlord in definite proportions which vary from country to country[9]. Thus, in respect of surplus appropriation, Marx held this as a sort of 'halfway home between pure profit and pure rent'. This was levelled as the expression of 'more or less a semi-feudal society[10]. The landlords here are cost participating semifeudal landlords.

Innovations and the semifeudal landlords

Contrary to normal expectations, the participation of the landlords in the cost, which introduces a profit element in the surplus appropriated by them, is not found to be strongly associated with the output raising innovations, Assuming that the adoption of the HYV crops is the expression of the such an innovation, we find that only in 30.3 percent of cost sharing cases, the adoption of such a strategy was reported (Table A7). In formal terms, the contingency x^2 value describing the association between landlord's participation in cost and the adoption of the HYV crops assumes a value of 2.104. Hence, the hypothesis that there exists any association between the two attributs is rejected even at 5 per cent level of significance. (Table A5a)

Regarding the association between landlord's participation in the cost and his involvement in the decision making process of the farm, the picture is somewhat different. A contingency x^2 value of 12.79 permits one to conclude that the association is significant at 1 percent level of significance (Table A5a).

Given that the big landlords have no scarcity of investible surplus, this, together with the previous finding as regards the poor response of the landlords vis-a-vis the adoption of output raising innovations, suggests that the semi-feudal landlords who participate largely in the decision making process, are not generally induced to adopt the output raising innovations. At the same time, given a weak asset base of the tenants, even the minimum utilisation of the soil often makes it

9. Ibid, pp 783

10. Ibid, pp. 769.

necessary for the landowners to participate in the cost. Under such a situation, the landlords find it advisable to limit their cost participation to traditional crops only, where the cash requirement is small. In other words, they are not inclined to accept agriculture as the major area of investment.

Such a phenomenon could be explained in several ways. Bhaduri (1973) tried to explain this in terms of the existence of interlinkage between tenancy and credit conditions. We shall reserve our comments on the empirical validity of his explanation with respect to our data until we consider the credit conditions pertaining to the tenants, which we take up in the next section. At this stage, we limit our observation only to the fact that an output raising innovations under the leadership of the big landlord did not register any significant progress in the tenurial holdings visited by us.

Further comments on Innovations

Let us now try to consider the problem of adopting the output raising innovation from the point of view of the tenants. In table 7, it is indicated that the predominant type of combination is 'F', where the landlords do not participate in the cost, and the production decisions are taken exclusively by the tenants. 51.85 percent of the total cases belong to this category. We find that the adoption of the HYV crops is very poor there; only 14.29 percent of these cases adopted such a strategy, leaving 85.71 percent of such tenants under traditional cropping arrangements. A probable explanation is that most of such tenants, as pointed out earlier, are people with weak land (and therefore other asset) base. They can not afford to go in for the adoption of the HYV crops which have cash requirements higher than that in traditional ones and which they themselves can not procure. Their landlords, typical absentees in every respect vis-a-vis production, remain satisfied with ground rent alone. Such a situation is not conducive to the adoption of the new agricultural strategy.

Considering the last element of each combination of table 7, it is found that the tenurial arrangement most conducive to the adoption of the HYV crops is either 'A' or 'D' type situation. 'A' type arrangement implies, that the landlords are becoming enterprising, they are taking up agriculture as the profitable area of investment and the tenurial system is not an obstacle to such a growth. D type arrangement, on the other hand implies that land is being leased out to such persons who can invest for the adoption of the HYV crops. But both these types account for a very small percentage of the cases. As a result, the incidence of the adoption of the HYV crops remains very poor in our sample. Only 22.2 percent of the total households were found to adopt such output raising innovations.

Table A7 : Participation of Landlords in Production Decision & Cost

Participation in production decision		Participation in cost: Participates	Does not participate	Total
		A	B	
Landlord only	T	6(7.41)*	1(1.23)*	7(8.64)*
	HYV crop	4(22.22)**	0(0.00)**	4(22.22)**
	%	66.67	0.00	57.14
		C	D	
Joint	T	10.(12.35)*	5(6.17)*	15(18.52)*
	HYV crop	3(16.67)**	2(11.11)**	5(27.78)**
	%	30.00	40.00	33.33
		E	F	
Tenant only	T	17(20.98)*	42(51.85)*	59(72.84)*
	HYV crops	3(16.67)**	6(33.33)**	9(50.00)**
	%	17.65	14.29	15.25
Total	T	33(40.74)*	48(59.25)*	81
	HYV crop	10(55.56)**	8(44.44)**	18
	%	30.30	16.658	22.22

* p.c. of total 181 cases
** p.c. of 18 cases adopting the HYV crop
T = Total cases

V

Private Lending

From the discussions of previous sections, it is found that non-legalised share cropping arrangement fixing the share ratios mostly in favour of the big landowners and a poor adoption of the output raising innovations by the landowners are the two important features of the tenurial practices we happened to observe in the district. Bhaduri (1973) explained the poor adoption of the output-raising innovations by the landowners under such share tenancy arrangements in terms of the existence of interlinkage between tenancy and credit condition. With a view to judging the empirical relevance of such a proposition, in this section we consider the credit conditions prevailing in the field area.

Table 8 describes the credit position of the tenant households. It is found that about 80 percent of the tenants in the credit market are receivers of loan. Indirectly this implies that there exists a high degree of credit requirement by the tenants – a point justifiably highlighted by both the policy makers and the academicians.

A classwise break up of tenants, however, indicates that there is a tendency for systematic variation in the behaviour of tenants, regarding the entry in the credit market. It is found that higher the land base (ownership wise) higher the participation in the credit market as receivers of loan (column 6). The poorer people are found to participate less, obviously not because their credit requirement is lower; they get less loan because they are less credit-worthy - the collateral that they can offer is often unacceptable to the lenders[11].

Even after the much advertised 'massive expansion' of institutional credit (mainly from Commercial Banks and Co-operative Credit Societies) in Nadia[12], we find that the private agencies still hold their sway in the credit market. Thus, only 24 percent of the loan receiving tenants reported to depend exclusively on credit in-

---

11. The leased-in land does not usually serve as collateral for institutional credits. In recent years, the government of West Bengal is trying to make arrangement with the commercial banks so that the leased-in land could serve as sureties against bank advances. Not much progress has been registered on this issue. For private credits, leasehold lands have no special significance except for those lenders who also maintain the landlease contract with the borrower.

12. It is claimed that there has been massive expansion of Institutional-credits, *viz.*, credits from commercial banks, co-operative credit societies and land development banks in recent years. Thus, population per branch of commercial banks in 1977 is 35.5 thousand, whereas in 1969, the corresponding figure was 1.95 lakh. More than 85 percent of advances to Nadia (about Rs. 6.36 crores in 1977) are in the priority sector. Co-operative credit societies provided loans worth of Rs. 523.87 lakh in 1977. The land development bank provided loans worth of Rs. 217.50 lakh in 1977. It is claimed that every village has been brought under the coverage of co-operatives.

stitutions. The corresponding figure for private sources is 34. Again, considering the persons who take loan both from private and institutional sources, we find that institutions served 28 such persons. All told, therefore, 51 percent of the tenants depend on institutions as sources of credit. The comparable figure for private sources, however, is 60. Thus, on both counts, we find that the private agencies have an edge over the institutional sources.

However, this information also support the view that the absolute domination of private lenders in the rural credit market is a matter of earlier days. In our cases, we find that the large majority of the tenants try to combine both private and institutional agencies as sources of credit.

The classwise breakup of institutional credit indirectly supports the conventional belief that the institutional credit tends to be distributed in the same proportion as the landholding among agricultural households. Column 7 of table 8 reveals that higher the landbase (ownershipwise), higher the percentage of people receiving loans from the institutions. While appreciating that poorer the people, lower the access to organised credit because of the relative unsoundness of the collateral that could be supplied against loans, it will be too much to infer from what we have shown that there exist an inverse relation between the land base and the degree of dependence on private credit for the tenants included in the sample. Column 8 of table 8 suggests just the opposite. Here we find that higher the landbase, higher the percentage of people depending on private agencies, too.

Assuming a higher rate of interest for credit from private sources, informations of Column 7 and 8 taken together suggest that the institutional credit, even when available, is not sufficient to meet the credit requirements of even the creditworthy households. Under such a situation, people find it imperative to approach the private lenders. As a result, the percentage of tenants tied to the private lenders becomes high.

Production loan, Consumption loan

For the 51 cases reporting involvement in credit from private sources, the typewise break-up of the loan is given in table A9. We classified loans into two broad categories: consumption loan and production loan. We have defined consumption loan as credit taken

Table A8 : Description of the Sources of Credit for Various Classes of the Tenant Households

Class of tetants	Persons receiving credit from			Persons receiv-ing cre-dit from all sources	Total tenants repor-ted	(4) as p.c. of (5)	(1) + (3) as p.c. of (5)	(2) + (3) as p.c. of (5)
	Institution only	Private only	Both Inst. & private					
	(1)	(2)	(3)	(4)	(5)	(6)	(7)	(8)
Landless	2	6	2	10	17	58.82	23.53	47.06
Marginal	9	14	15	38	47	80.85	51.06	61.70
Small	4	2	9	15	17	88.24	76.47	64.71
Medium to rich	1	1	2	4	4	100	75	75.00
Total	16	23	28	67	85	78.82	51.76	60.00

Note : Marginal farmer : Size of owned land not exceeding one hectare. Small Farmer : Size of owned land lying between 1 & 2 hectares
Medium or rich : Size of owned land exceeding 2 hectares

either in cash or in kind during any season of the year (not necessarily during the pre-harvest lean seasons) for purposes other than meeting production expenses. In otherwords, we did not distinguish here between 'consumption loan' from landlords and other unproductive general purpose loans. Again, by the term 'production loan', we define such loans as might be taken by the household for meeting the cost of circulating capital only (taken either in cash or in kind). We found two cases of loans for fixed asset building (from 'medium to rich' group). We did not include them in this study.

Table A9 : Typewise Break up of Credit from Private Sources

Class of tenants	Consumption loan	Production loan	Both	Total
Landless	4(50.00)	2(25.00)	2(25.00)	8(100.00)
Marginal	7(24.13)	13(44.82)	9(31.03)	29(100.00)
Small	5(45.45)	5(45.45)	1(9.09)	11(100.00)
Medium to Rich	0(0.00)	3(100.00)	0(0.00)	3(100.00)
Total	16(31.37)	23(45.09)	12(23.53)	51(100.00)

Note : Figures in parenthesis denote the percentages.

About 45 per cent of the cases having involvement in credits from private sources was found to have taken loans for production purposes only. The corresponding figure for consumption loans is about 31 percent. Considering also the cases that report involvement in both production and consumption loans, the total cases reporting to incur consumption loans increases to 55 per cent. But then, the figure is again lower than the corresponding score of the group reporting to have taken production loans (about 70 percent). For the tenant households as a whole, therefore, production loans dominate.

There is again a significant variation in the behaviour of various classes of tenants regarding the involvement in production and consumption loans. At the one extreme, there are 'medium to rich' farmers who do not require any consumption loan from private sources. At the other extreme, however, we find that 75 percent of the credit-worthy landless tenants reported having incurred consumption loans. Of the indebted tenants belonging to small and marginal groups, 55 per cent reported to have taken consumption loans from private sources. For landless to small farmers as a whole, we find that about 59 per cent of the indebted households required consumption loans.

Landlord as source of loan

In a situation of inadequately developed organised credit institution, it is expected that a landlease contract will be linked with a credit contract in case of poor tenants, because in the absence of other sureties, tenancy contract might serve as an acceptable collateral to the landlords[13]. In case of tenant households visited by us, we did not find much evidence in support of that hypothesis. Out of 35 cases of production loans, landlords were mentioned as sources of credit only in 12 cases. (table A10)

Table A10 : Sourcewise Breakup of Production Loan (From Private Sources)

Class of tenants	Landlord		Nonlandlord*	Total
	Without interest	With interest		
Landless	1	1	2	4
Marginal	4	3	15	22
Small	1	1	4	6
Medium to Big	1	0	2	3
Total	7	5	23	35

For explanation, see the text.

Bardhan and Rudra (1980) and Rudra (1975) have reported that a significant proportion of West Bengal landlords provide interest free loans for their tenants. The reality we experienced in Nadia fully corroborates their view. In 7 out of 12 cases of landlords giving production loans, we found that no interest was charged on the principal.

Of these tenants, 28 were reported to have incurred consumption loans from private sources. The participation of landlord as loan giver is again very poor. Only in 6 cases, landlords are found to supply consumption loans to their tenants. Half of these cases were again interest free loans (Table All). Considering both consumption and production loans, we find that the landlords served as sources of

13. Not necessarily the landlords included in the sample.

credit only in 18 cases. Out of these 18 cases, 10 were interest-free loans. Even without considering the structure of interest rate for the cases where interest is charged, one may, therefore, safely reject the proposition that the associated landlords usually maintain the usury nexus with the tenants, that dampens the incentive to increase production through productive investments.

Table A11 : Sourcewise Breakup of Consumption Loan

Class of tenants	Landlord		Friends & Relatives		Non land-lord*	Total
	With interest	Without interest	With interest	Without interest		
Landless	1	2	1	1	1	6
Marginal	2	1	1	2	10	16
Small	0	0	0	2	4	6
Medium to big	0	0	0	0	0	0
Total	3	3	2	5	15	28

* For explanation, see the text.

Considering the sources of production and consumption loans for various classes of tenants, we find that the landless tenants, who generally have no other collateral than the tenancy contracts to offer against loans, find their landlords the most important single source of credit (5out of 10). For the other classes of tenants, the story is completely different. Only 13 out of 53 cases reported landlords as the source of loan; for others, the most important loan givers were the nonlandlords (35 out of 53). No small or 'medium to rich' farmer reported landlords as the source of consumption loan. (Incidentally, no 'medium to rich' farmer was reported to have incurred any consumption loan). We encountered only one case of interest free production loan from landlords, taken by a 'medium to rich' farmer. We suppose, this is just an isolated case.

Thus, we find that the interlinkage between the tenancy contract and the credit contract is not very powerful in case of the households visited by us. For the landless households, the chain is somewhat important. For other classes of tenants, it is quite negligible.

Before we enter into other aspects of the credit conditions, we would like to mention an interesting point. Table 11 indicates that 'friends and relatives' and not the landlords are the most important sources of interest-free loans. In fact, the category of 'friends and relatives' was found to provide loans in 7 out of 28 cases of consumption loans, out of which 5 were interest free. The landlords, on the other hand, provide interest free credits in only 3 out of 6 cases of consumption loans.

This finding also contradicts the notion that the friends and relatives often provide credit with similar terms and conditions, as those of the professional moneylenders[14].

Non Landlord Sources

The large majority of the tenants found local traders, professional people (e.g. school teachers with small land base, village doctors, etc) professional money lenders (with small land base) and others (e.g. grocery owners, fellow farmers) as the sources of both production and consumption loan. This credit has a highly personalised character, i.e. the relation between the lender and the borrower is a highly personalised one. The loan is sanctioned against no sureties. Of course, the amount involved is not also very high, the credit is often a short-term one - the average turnover period being roughly one quarter of the year. The importance of such sources in the credit market is revealed in tables A10 and A11.

Of these sources, traders are by far the most important. They account for 10 out of 23 cases of non-landlord sources of production loan, and 7 out of 15 cases of such consumption loans. Professional people and professional moneylenders have almost equal importance. Grocery owners and fellow farmers ('others' in our category) do not seem to matter much in the rural credit. They account for 2 cases both in the category of production loans and consumption loans (Table A12).

Modes of Repayment

In a pioneering contribution on the credit situation in West Bengal, Rudra (1975) identified 7 different modes of repayment in rural Bengal. He also observed that the concept of 'Interest rate in the proper sense of the word prevails especially for loans obtained from money lenders or other loan giving agencies as well as for general

---

14. See Kurup, T.V.N.(1976)

purpose loans[15]. We subscribe largely to Rudra's view.

We encountered all Rudra's categories except 'Money to crop(b)' type mode of repayment[16]. In addition, we observed 2 cases of traders' loans given in the form of fertiliser against which cash repayment with some interest was sought. We categorised it as 'other commodity to money type' mode of repayment.

Table A12 : Description of Production and Consumption Loans from Various Non-Landlord Sources

Sources[(a)]	Production loan	Consumption loan[(b)]
Trader	10	7
Professional people	5	3
Professional Money lenders	6	3
Others	2	2
Total	23	15

(a) For further details, see the text.
(b) Including loans for general purposes.

Table A13 and A14 describe the modes of repayment of production and consumption loans in such cases where interest payment is involved. We find that out of 28 cases of loans for production purposes, there were 21 cases of cash credit and none of them was supplied by the landlords. In case of consumption loans also we find that 12 out of 20 cases were cash credits and all of them were supplied by the non landlords. A closer examination reveals that most of these cash credits are supplied not by the traders but by the professional people and professional money lenders. Thus, out of 21 cases of cash credit fo production purposes, traders accounted for only 8 cases. In case of consumption loans also, traders provided cash credit for 4 tenants only, the rest depended exclusively on professional people and professional moneylenders.

---

15. Rudra. A. (1975): pp 1053

16. A specified quantity of crop to be repaid irrespective of price. In Rudra's (1975) survey also, such cases were not found to be very frequent.

Table A13 : Modes of Repayment : Production Loan

Modes	Lenders					
	Landlord	Trader	Profes-sional people	Profes-sional Money lenders	Others	Total
Money to money		2	3	6	1	12
Other commodity to crop	4*	-	-	-	-	4
Money to crop (a)	-	6**	2	-	1	9
Other commodity to money	-	2***	-	-	-	2
Crop to labour	1	-	-	-	-	1
Total	5	10	5	6	2	28(e)

Notes (1) * Fertiliser to crop
** Commodity involves : June
*** Fertiliser to Money
(e) Excluding 7 cases of interest free loans given by the landlords.

(2) For explanation of the modes, see Rudra (1975); also our text. We did not encounter 'money to crop (b)' type mode of repayment as mentioned in Rudra (1975). Instead, we encountered 'other commodity to money' type mode of repayment. For discussion, see the text.

The incidence of cash credit from private sources for production purposes should not, however, be overemphasised. It was observed that such loans were small and lumpy, required to meet additional wage expenses for quick completion of weeding (in case of jute and aus paddy) occasioned by incessant rain for 2 to 3 days in late Jaistha or early Asar (some time in July). In some cases, these loans were required for purchasing insecticides and fertilisers from such traders who do not find it safe to lend these inputs against unsatisfactory collaterals.

Cash credit for consumption purposes should be better described as general purpose loans, including loans for consumption purposes, because it was observed that such loans were required for meeting various urgent domestic requirements such as purchase of medicine, meeting travelling expenses and outstanding grocery bills, apart from purchasing cereals.

Table A14 : Modes of Repayment : Consumption Loan

Modes/	Sources Friends relatives	Landlord	Trader	Profess-ional people	Profes-sional moneylenders	Others	Total
Money to money	1	-	1	3	3	1	9
Crop to crop(1)	-	2	1	-	-	-	3
Crop to crop(2)	-	-	1*	-	-	-	1
Money to crop (a)	-	-	3	-	-	-	3
Crop to labour	-	1	-	-	-	-	1
Other commodity to money	-	-	-	-	-	1**	1
Could not be ascertained	1	-	1	-	-	-	2
Total	2	3	7	3	3	2	20(e)

Notes (1) *Commodity involved: Jute: ** General grocery items
(e) Excluding 8 cases of interest free loans.
(2) For explanation, see footnote 2 of table 13.

Table A15 :Monthly Interest on Cash Repayment of Production and Consumption Loans

Rate of Interest/ (per cent)	Lenders Friends & relatives	Traders	Profes-sional people	Profes-sional money lenders	Others	Total
1 - 5	-	1	-	-	-	1
6 - 10	-	2	4	5	1	12
11 - 15	-	-	1	3	1	5
20	-	-	-	1	1	2
Could not be ascertained	1	2	1	-	-	4
Total cases	1	5	6	9	3	24

The rate of interest on cash repayment of credit is exorbitantly high. 12 out of 24 cases of cash repayment reported a monthly rate of return between 6 and 10 per cent. Another 7 cases reported an even higher rate. The professional people, the professional moneylenders, and others who supply most of such cash credits and receive most of the repayment in cash bank on such a high return on short term advances supplied against no sureties. It seems that such a practice is the most remunerative way of parting with the liquidities in the short run.

A high rate of return on such short run investments should, logically speaking, induce other prospective creditors to enter into the credit market so that the rate of interest is reduced in the long run. This, however, is not true. A high rate of interest increases the risk of default that could effectively be countered only through a highly personalised character of credit that could be maintained only by the lenders with superior social and economic power. Such conditions are not satisfied by many. Hence, a monopoly power is enjoyed by these lenders. This monopoly power again explains such a high rate of interest.

Excluding five cases where traders were found to accept cash repayment of loans, we find that in other cases the traders insist on repayment in kind. There are 9 cases where the creditors received jute against cash advances. The calculation was $M = Q_2 P^1$; M is the amount of cash, Q_2 is the amount of jute at price P^1 where $P^1 + d =$ prevailing market price $(d > o)$. thus the traders' control over the produce could be maintained by the operation of credit chains, and that too at a lower cost. Two cases of fertiliser advances, however, did not indicate such a pattern. They were to be repaid in terms of money with a rate of interest which, of course, was high. Traders were found to make crop advances only in two cases of consumption loan with the condition of repayment in terms of crops again, with some additional amount of crop as interest. Thus, the major interest of the traders, as we find, is to control output by making advances both against the consumption and production requirements of tenants.

The participation of landlords in the credit market, as we have already seen, is very poor. A significant portion of their advances is again interest free. There were only 5 cases of landlords making production advances. Three cases of consumption advances made by them were also reported. In no such case is cash repayment insisted on. Repayment in terms of labour appeared in 2 cases; 6 out of 8 cases reported a mode of repayment in terms of crops. Four of such loans were occasioned by fertiliser advances. The amount of commodity repaid was

$$Q_2 = \frac{F}{2} \cdot \frac{P_3}{P_2}$$

where F is the fertiliser used in the land under tenancy, P_3 is the price of fertiliser and P_2 is the price of HYV rice at post harvest. The traditional pattern of crop advances taken as consumption loan is conspicuous by its virtual non-existence. Only 2 cases reported a repayment in terms of paddy against paddy loans, with a kind rate of return. The rate is not related to any unit of time. It is related to the principal in a once-for-all fashion. The rate observed was 50 percent of the principal in both the cases.

VI

Conclusion

The empirical findings reported here reveal some important phenomena. In the first place, the tenurial arrangements were found to be associated with backward production conditions; a typical tenant did not take up the new agricultural strategy; cost sharing as an investment proposition was also missing from the pattern of behaviour of the landlords. A non-legalised sharecropping arrangement that assures a high share of the produce for the landowners, wielding semifeudal authority over the tenants in a near stagnant agrarian economy, is the typical reality with respect to the observed households. No neat model on the line of differential risk aversion or varying bargaining power of individual lessors and lessees seems to be applicable to such an economy.

At the same time, the data contradict some crucial formulations of Bhaduri (1973). The typical landlord that we came across did not, however, enter into usury practices with his tenants who nevertheless needed both production and consumption loans. In fact, no strong interlinkage could be found between tenancy contracts and credit contracts. The credit market was found to be dominated by the non-landlord loan givers (e.g., traders, professional moneylenders, etc.) and not by the landlords as assumed by Bhaduri.

A model on agrarian backwardness should therefore be based on some explanatory factors other than the interlinkage between credit conditions and tenurial arrangements.

REFERENCES

1. Bardhan. P. and Rudra, A. Terms and Conditions of Share Cropping Contracts: An Analysis of Village Survey Data in India, *Journal of Development Studies,* Vol.16, April, 1980.
2. Bardhan, P. and Srinivasan, T.N. Crop sharing Tenancy in Agriculture : A Theoretical and Empirical Analysis, *American Economic Review,* Vol.61. No.1, 1971
3. Bell, C. and Zusman, P. A Bargaining Theoretic Approach to Cropsharing Contracts, *American Economic Review,* Vol. 66, No.4, 1976.
4. Bhaduri, A. Agricultural Backwardness Under Semifeudalism, *Economic Journal,* Vol.88, March, 1973.
5. Bharadwaj, J.K. *On Some Issues of Method in the Analysis of Social Changes*, University of Mysore, 1980.
6. Cheung, S.N.S. *the Theory of Share Tenancy*, Chicago University Press, 1969.
7. Godelier, Maurice. *Rationality and Irrationality in Economics*, New Left Books London, 1972.
8. Government of India, Department of Statistics, *National Sample Survey 26th Round Report 215, West Bengal,* Vol. 1.
9. Green, Francis and Nore, Petter (ed). *Economics: An Anti-Text*. The Macmillan Press, London, 1977.
10. Johnson. D.G. *Resource Allocation Under Share Contract, Journal of Political Economy,* Vol. 58, No. 2, 1950.
11. Kurup, T.V.N. Price of Rural Credit : An Empirical Analysis of Kerala, *Economic and Political Weekly,* Vol. 11, No. 27, 1976.
12. Marx, Karl. *Capital,* Vol. 3, Foreign Language Publishing House, Moscor, 1962.
13. Newbery, D.G.M. Cropsharing Tenancy in Agriculture: A Comment, *American Economic Review*, Vol. 64, No. 6, 1974.

    —— Risksharing Sharecropping and Uncertain Markets, *Review of Economic Studies, October, 1977.*
14. Parthasarathy G. 'West Godavari, Andhra Pradesh' included in Changes in Rice Farming in Selected Areas of Asia, *IRRI*, Philippines, 1975.
15. Rao, C.H.H. *Technological Changes and Distribution of Gains in Indian Agriculture*, Institute of Economic Growth, Delhi, 1975.
16. Reid, Joseph. *Sharecropping dand Agricultural Uncertainty*, Economic Development and Cultural Changes, April, 1976.
17. Rudra, A. Loans as Part of Agrarian Relations: Some Results of a Preliminary Survey in West Bengal, *Economic and Political Weekly, July 12, 1975.*

    —— Sharingcropping arrangements in West Bengal, *Economic and Political Weekly*, September 27, 1975(a).
18. Stiglitz, J.E. Incentives and Risksharing in Share-cropping, *Review of Economic Studies,* Vol. 41, No. 1, 1974.
19. *West Bengal Land Reforms Act, 1955 (with ammendments upto 1980)*, Kamal Law House, Calcutta, 1980.

APPENDIX II

URBAN GROWTH WITHOUT URBANISATION

Introduction

A high rate of urban[1] growth[2] does not necessarily imply a fast urbanisation.[3] This is particularly true when the urban centres experience a dwarfed economic growth arresting the effectiveness of the 'urban pull' factor of the population movement. The present chapter examines this hypothesis with reference to Nadia, a small but populous district[4] of West Bengal situated in the eastern plains of the state, bordering Bangladesh.

A decaying district in the early part of this century in terms of the growth of population, Nadia experienced a high influx of refugees following the partition of Bengal. As we shall show below, this exogeneous factor brought about a high rate of urban growth and a fast urbanisation during the early years following the partition. During the next two decades, the pace of urban growth remained moderately high, but this was not coupled with even a nominal rise in urbanisation. Urban development, in case of Nadia, thus became merely a demographic illusion during that period.

This chapter attempts to explain such a strange phenomenon in terms of the dwarfed growth of the urban economic activities. It has been observed that during the first two decades after independence, there had been a relative decline of the 'services sector', the largest employment generating sector of urban Nadia, in terms of work force absorption. By and large, this was not compensated by the growth of secondary activities. As a result, instead of migration from rural areas a voluntary response to greater economic opportunities (the 'urban pull' factor), a 'push-back' of work-force to primary sector (mainly as agricultural labourer) that would arrest the pace of urbanisation, had been taking place in the district until the 'urban pull' factor became operative again in 1971-81.

Urban growth in Nadia before the partition of Bengal

During the first three decades of this century, the pace of urban growth was very poor in Nadia.[5] As the table-1 indicates, the urban population increased at an average rate of just 2.58 per cent per decade during this period. This is quite low particularly when one notes that the corresponding all India rate was 9.27 per cent per decade.[6] Considering the demographic performance of urban Nadia vis-a-vis that of its rural hinterland, the performance, however, does not seem to be as deplorable as a comparison with all India data indicates. Since the late 19th century, according to various census reports, Nadia was a 'decaying district' in terms of demographic performance. During the first three decades of this century, as our table-1 indicates, the decaying tendency was quite apparent–the district population during this period decreased at an average rate of 2.16 per cent per decade, the rate of decrease in the rural areas being 2.72 per cent. The decay of the river system, the growing poverty of the soil, extremely low health together with the prevalent land tenure system of *utbondi*[7] which introduced insecurity of tenure were the reason for the deplorable state of agriculture and the consequent large scale migration from rural areas. This largely explains the absolute decline of the population in the rural areas. The absolute decline is also explained by high death rates caused by the frequent out-break of epidemics and near-famine conditions in the rural areas.[8] Be that as it may, in the background of absolute decline in population in the rural areas, the relative performance of the urban areas in not as deplorable as it seems to be. In fact, during the second and the third decades of this century, there was a rising trend of urbanisation in the district as the table-5 indicates.

The rate of urban growth during 1931-1941 was 35.43 per cent, a high rate compared to the pervious period. The growth rate was 13.83 per cent in the rural areas and that of the district was 16.40 per cent. All these rates are well above the rates attained during any of the first three decades of this century. While a part of such a rise was due to 'bogus inflation in the 1941 census count' (Census, 1951 p xiii), there are grounds to believe that the district experienced a moderate to high rate of repopulation. The census report cites immigration from other districts along with the improvement in the health situation of the district as a consequence of the implementation of several minor drainage schemes, as the reasons for such a rise in the population.

The influx of refugees and the urban growth

The highest ever urban growth in the district was recorded during the next decade when as a consequence of the partition of Bengal, there had been an influs of refugees from East Pakistan to Nadia. During 1946-51, according to the Census estimate, 426907 displaced persons migrated from East Pakistan to Nadia. This was about 37.29 per cent of the total population of the district in 1951. According to one calculation, the net inflow to the district during 1941-51 had been about 344462 persons.[9] This is about 30 per cent of the estimated population of the district in 1951.

It seems that the migration from East Pakistan has a tremendous impact on the demography of the district. The decennian growth rate for the district jumped to 36.25 per cent, The rural population increased by 29.39 per cent and the urban population scored a record rise of 78.96 per cent after the partition of Bengal. Such a rise can not be explained but by large scale immigration during 1941-1951, given the fact that the cyclone of 1942 and the famine that caused the epidemic of 1943-1944 had reduced the natural population considerably during this period.

Since the census data do not provide us with the destination-wise break-up of the immigrants, it is difficult to estimate the impact of refugee migration on the urban growth of Nadia on the basis of the census data. However, there are two official studies on the displaced persons that might be utilised for this purpose. The first is a report 'On the Sample Survey for Estimating the Socio-economic Characteristics of Displaced Persons Migrating from Eastern Pakistan to the State of West Bengal' (Government of West Bengal, 1951 (a)). The second is a study 'On the Rehabilitation of Refugees' conducted by the State Statistical Bureau (Government of West Bengal, 1956). According to the first report, 403804 persons had immigrated to the district between 1946 and 1951 of whom 67696 settled in the urban areas (Report 1951 a, p. 13). The second report records the number of immigrants during 1946-1955 as 386500, 77900 of them having settled in the urban areas (Report 1956; p. 90-91). On the basis of the Report (1951 (a)), the estimated urban growth due to refugee migration is 58.22 per cent. The percentage becomes 66.99 (for a period of fifteen years - 1941-1955) if we consider the number of immigrants on the basis of the second (1956) report (see table 2). On the basis of these estimates, it is reasonable to conclude that the contribution of migration from East Pakistan to the urban growth of Nadia during this decade was quite high. In fact, there are reasons to believe that immigration contributed much more than the natural factors in explaining the variation in urban population during this period. On the basis of the census data and the Report 1951(a), one understands that the growth of urban population due to natural factors is 20.74 per cent, the contribution of migration being about three times higher.

The Growth pattern at disaggregate level

The urban growth pattern in five important towns[10] of the district have been presented in table-3. All these towns, except Nabadwip, registered either depopulation or virtual stagnation in terms of urban growth during the first three decades of this century. The uninterrupted urban growth in Nabadwip is partly explained by the existence of a stable services sector associated with tourism on account of the continuing importance of the town as a Hindu pilgrim centre. Another reason for such a stable urban growth is the agricultural prosperity of the adjacent rural areas of Burdwan with fertile land that induced double-cropping even in the early 20th century.[11] This agricultural prosperity is a powerful factor which sustained the important of the town as a trade centre. Such favourable factors were, however, absent in case of other towns. Trade and other tertiary activities associated with the primary sector could not flourish in any significant manner in those towns because of the poor state of agriculture in their respective rural hinterlands. Tourism and such other favourable factors were also absent in case of those towns.

For each of these towns, the highest rate of urban growth was recorded during 1941-1951. Among the urban centres, however, a considerable variation in the growth rates of population have also been observed. Thus, Krishnanagar and Santipur, the two traditionally populous towns of the district, experienced a moderate rise, while Chakdaha, a town with an average decennial rate of growth around 1.13 per cent recorded 179.80 per cent rise in population during this period.

TABLE 1: **Percentage (Decade) Variation in Population : 1901-1981**

Decade	Nadia Urban	Nadia Rural	Nadia Dist.
1901-11	0.52	0.34	0.36
1911-21	-0.29	-9.20	-8.28
1921-31	7.51	0.66	1.43
1931-41	35.43	13.83	16.40
1941-51	78.96	29.39	36.25
1951.61	51.53	49.21	49.64
1961-71	32.57	29.64	30.14
1971-81	52.65	29.51	33.86

Sources : Census of India, 1971, Series 22, W.B., Part II A;
Census of India, 1961, Series 23, W.B., Paper I of 1981, Supplement.

TABLE 2: **Immigration during 1946-1955 and Urbanisation in Nadia.**

1.	Urban population in 1941 (U_1):	116284	
2.	Rural population in 1941(R_1):	724017	
		Estimate 1	*Estimate 2*
3.	Reported migration to the urban areas (M_2) :	67696	77900
4.	Reported migration to the rural areas (M_1) :	336108	308600
5.	Per cent increase in urban population due to immigrant: $\frac{M_2}{U_1} \times 100$	58.22	66.99
6.	Per cent increase in rual population due to immigrants: $\frac{M_1}{R_1} \times 100$	46.42	42.62
7.	Per cent urbanisation due to immigrants :	8.06	9.27

Notes: Estimate 1: Estimated on the basis of Report 1951 (a).
Estimate 2: Estimated on the basis of Report 1955.
M_1 = Refugees migrating to rural areas.
M_2 = Refugees Migrating to urban areas.
R_1 = 1941 population in rural areas.
U_1 = 1941 population in urban areas.

Sources: Census of India 1971. Series 22. W.B. District Census Handbook. Nadia; Report 1951(a); Report 1955.

The contribution of the influx of refugees to such a sudden rise in the growth rate is considerably high, as the per cent increases in urban population due to immigration in 5 leading towns of the district, estimated on the basis of the Report (1956) indicates (table-4). One important finding of the table is that the urban growth due to immigration in case of Chakdaha is abnormally high, so much so that the new Chakdaha can be considered to be a product of the partition of Bengal. For the other towns, as an explanatory factor for urban growth, the natural rise in population continues to be a powerful factor. The impact of immigration seems to be the lowest in Santipur, a very old municipal town in the Western part of the district.

The Pace of Urbanisation

Table-5 describes the pace of urbanisation in the district during this century. At 1901, about 10 per cent of the population of the district lived in the urban areas. Up to 1931, the per cent variation in the percentage of population in the urban areas was not high, as the column 3 of the table-5 indicates. However, the data do indicate a slow growth of urbanisation during this period. The slowest rate of growth was recorded during the first decade of this century.

The urbanisation assumed a faster pace during 1931-1941 and attained the peak during 1941-1951. In 1951 18.18 per cent of the population had been living in the urban areas. During this decade, there had been a 31.36 per cent increase in the urban percentage of the population. With reference to 1931, the pace of urbanisation was as high as 52.90 per cent.

Before 1947, migration from other districts to Nadia had always been a rare phenomenon. A rise in the percentage of urban population could, therefore, be explained in terms of a lower natural growth rate of the rural population and/or an intra-district migration from rural areas to urban centres. In fact, the growth of urbanisation during the second and the third decade of this century when migration to Nadia had been a rare phenomenon,[12] is largely explained by these factors. One could argue that better living conditions in the urban areas induced a higher natural rise in population by reducing the death rate. On the other hand, frequent outbreak of epidemics in the rural areas, besides causing a higher death rate, induced migration to towns, because the civic and health amenities had been better in the urban areas. Such factors might explain a relative decline in rural population, and a consequent rise of urbanisation in the district.

But the sudden rise in the rate of urbanisation during 1941-1951 can not be explained in terms of these factors alone, because the rise in urbanisation was concommittant to an influx of refugees from outside the state. The importance of such an exogeneous factor can be appreciated if one notes that in such a case, even under the assumption of no intra-district migration and equality of growth proportions of natural population in urban and rural areas, a rise in the percentage of urban population is logically possible. This could occur if the refugees' migration to rural areas (M_1) as proportion to the original population in the rural areas (R_1) be less than the migration of refugees to urban (M_2) areas as proportion to the original population in the urban areas (U_1).

In case of Nadia, as the table-2 indicates, M_1/R_1 was less than M_2/U_1 according to both of the alternative estimates. Thus, there are grounds to believe that the migration from East Pakistan would have accelerated the pace of urbanisation even if the intra-district migration to urban areas and the tendency of higher net reproduction rate in the urban areas had been absent in the district.

The extent of urbanisation due to refugee influx, when other factors favouring urbanisation are also taken into consideration, is given by the proportion of immigrants to urban areas to the total population of the district. In 1951 this was between 5.91 per cent and 6.80 per cent which is quite high (between 32.50 per cent and 37.40 per cent of per cent urban), given that the percentage of total population in the urban areas, i.e. per cent urban due to all the contributory factors, was just 18.18 in that year.

As table-5 indicates, there was a drastic fall in the tempo of urbanisation during the next two decades. The percentage of total population in the urban areas stagnated around 18.50 during this period. As a result, between 1951 and 1961 there was just an 1.27 per cent rise in the per cent urban population of the district; this is extremely poor compared to the corresponding rate attained in the previous decade. The pace of urbanisation was only 1.79 per cent during 1961-1971. Thus there was hardly any growth of urbanisation in the district during the two decades after the partition of Bengal.

TABLE 3: **Percent (Decade) Variation in Population in 5 leading Towns in Nadia**

Decade	Nabadwip	Krishnanagar	Chakdaha	Ranaghat	Santipur
1901-1911	14.71	-4.37	-15.59	12.65	-0.72
1911-1921	24.88	-4.97	5.78	-2.01	-7.16
1921-1931	21.03	8.85	-23.58	18.06	0.81
1931-1941	62.15	31.84	37.89	44.70	19.61
1941-1951	84.08	56.30	179.80	70.21	41.89
1951-1961	29.42	40.76	128.27	25.66	20.69
1961-1971	29.29	21.91	32.08	35.58	19.49
1971-1981	15.82	15.06	27.97	22.05	35.66

Source: Same as Table 1.

TABLE 4: **Immigration during 1946-1955 and per cent increase in population of 5 leading towns.**

Towns	Estimated per cent increase with respect to.		
	1941	1945	1951
Nabadwip	76.53	56.41	41.57
Krishnanagar	53.42	42.73	34.18
Chakdaha	283.22	169.32	101.22
Ranaghat	50.16	38.45	29.47
Santipur	34.30	28.79	24.17
Urban Nadia	66.99	50.07	37.43

Note: Average number of migrants per family in the urban area of the district X number of refugee families in the town in 1955 = Estimated migration in 1955.
Population of 1945 was interpolated.

Source: Census of India 1971, series 22, WB, Part II-A; Report, 1955.

TABLE 5: **Extent of Urbanisation : 1901-1981**

Decade	Per cent of total population in urban areas	Variation in per cent urban	Per cent variation in per cent urban
1901	10.30	-	-
1911	10.32	0.02	0.19
1921	11.22	0.90	8.72
1931	11.89	0.67	5.97
1941	13.84	1.95	16.40
1951	18.18	4.34	31.36
1961	18.41	0.23	1.27
1971	18.74	0.33	1.79
1981	21.59	2.85	15.21

Source : Same as Table 1.

As the last row of table-5 indicates, there had been a new spell of urbanisation in the district during 1971-'81. In the absence of any evidence in favour of either a spurt in intra-district migration from rural to urban areas or a higher natural rate of growth of urban population, this sudden rise in urbanisation might be explained, as in case of the rise in urbanisation during 1941-1951, by an exogeneous factor like large scale migration to urban Nadia from erstwhile Pakistan, following the Bangladesh war of 1971.

Summing up the finding one may, therefore, conclude that Nadia experienced a slow pace of urbanisation during the first three decades of this century. The tempo of urbanisation gained momentum during the next two decades until it reached the peak during the early years after the partition of Bengal. After that, there was a virtual stagnation in the tempo of urbanisation of the district although the decade rates of urban growth during 1951-1961 and 1961-1971 were substantially high (51.53 per cent and 32.57 per cent respectively). Thus, a high rate of urban growth coupled with a virtual stagnation in urbanisation, i.e. urban growth without urbanisation had become the reality of Nadia. There had been a slight revarsal of this tendency after the Bangladesh war when a high rate of urban growth was attended by a moderate rise in the rate of urbanisation in the district.

The decay of the old towns

In terms of the pace of urbanisation, the five leading towns of the district record a deplorable performance during the three decades following independence. It is true that in all these towns there was a moderate to high rate of urbanisation during 1941-1951. But by 1961, all towns except Chakdaha recorded negative rates of growth of urbanisation (Table 6, column 7). The de-urbanisation was strengthened further during the last decade when even Chakdaha reported a negative growth rate – the growth rate in case of Chakdaha declined to -3.85 per cent in 1971-1981 from 106.15 per cent during 1941-'51. An interesting feature of 1971-1981 is the re-urbanisation in Santipur where a 2.18 per cent growth rate was recorded after two consecutive decades of de-urbanisation.

TABLE 6: **Decay of the Old Towns of the Districts since 1951**

Towns	*Extent of Urbanisation**					*Variations***			
	1941	1951	1961	1971	1981	1941-1951	1951-1961	1961-1971	1971-1981
Nabadwip	3.64	4.92	4.25	4.22	3.68	1.28 ((35.16)	-0.67 (-13.62)	-0.03 (0.70)	-0.54 (-12.80)
Krishnanagar	3.81	4.37	4.11	3.85	3.31	0.56 (14.70)	-0.26 (8.75)	-0.26 (-6.33)	-0.54 (-14.03)
Chakdaha	0.65	1.34	2.04	2.08	2.00	0.69 (106.15)	0.70 (52.24)	0.04 (1.96)	-0.08 (-3.85)
Ranaghat	1.96	2.45	2.05	2.14	1.97	0.49 (25.00)	-0.40 (-16.33)	0.09 (4.39)	-0.17 (-7.94)
Santipur	3.56	3.70	2.99	2.74	2.80	0.14 (3.93)	-0.71 (-19.19)	-0.25 (-8.36)	0.06 (2.18)

* Rate of Urbanisation has been measured by the ratio of the population of the town with that of the district.
** Figures in brackets denote 'per cent variation'.
Source : Same as Table 1.

Assuming no variation in the intra-district natural growth rate of the population, table-6 indicates that the traditional urban centres of the district failed to attract people from the rural areas. In other words, the 'urban pull' factor had not been operative in the major urban centres of the district. There had been a relative decay of the old towns, a high rate of urban growth notwithstanding.

II

Urban growth without urbanisation may be due to a poor development of employment generating activities in urban areas compared to the rural hinterland, discouraging migration from rural areas. In this section, we examine this hypothesis in terms of the pace of workforce absorption in the urban sectors of the district during the three decades following 1951. We shall also consider the pace of work-force absorption during 1941-1951 in order to examine whether the 'urban pull' factor was responsible for large scale urbanisation after the partition of Bengal.

The analysis will be based on the relevant census data for the period (1941-1981).

The Problem of Inter-Census comparison

With the introduction of the 1961 scheme of classifying workers into economically active and other wise, the comparability with previous census data has become rather difficult. However, the census notes of 1961 (Census of India, 1961; Paper No. 1, 1961, pp. 389-394) outlines a procedure regarding the grouping of workers in previous census data in the form of standard categories of 1961. All such problem excepting that with the inter-census comparison of the female work-force could, therefore, be avoided. The problem with the inter-census comparison of female work-force is difficult to resolve. As we know, there has been a considerable rise in the work-force participation rate for females in 1961 census compared to that in 1951, probably due to a considerable variation in these two censuses in regard to the classification of unpaid family workers among the females. There is no suitable adjustment technique to take care of this problem. To be on the safe side, therefore, we found it advisable to drop it altogether from the purview of our discussion. The analysis that follows will, therefore, be based on the occupational pattern of the male work-force only.

There are some problems with the 1941 census also. Based on a two per cent sample (called Y-sample) of the original schedules, the distribution of the male-force for Nadia in 1941, as given in Census, 1941, does not contain any direct information about 'services in urban area'.[13] Since regionwise break up of such data which indicates the absorption of work-force in 'services' sector is not available for the district, a direct computation is not also possible. However, in order to pursue the inter-census comparison we have taken 'public administration and liberal art' as a proxy to 'services in urban areas', because most such activities are expected to concentrate in the urban areas. This has been selected as the only proxy because no other comparable occupational category seemed to have such a distinct urban bias.

There was another problem as regards the census data of 1941. On the basis of the extent of information on the 'industry including house-hold', it is not possible to get the division of the data between household manufacture and other than household manufacture, a division followed in 1961 and 1971 census studies. Such a problem also remains in case of 1951 census. In order to get comparability, we lumped 'household industry' with 'nonhousehold manufacture' in case of 1961 and 1971 census studies and formed a group, namely, 'industry including household' so that the inter-census comparison could be performed.

The 1941 census contains a category of 'insufficiently described' male work-force. Since no comparable data are available in the subsequent census studies, we drop it from the purview of our discussion.

The trend and structure of the sectoral distribution of work-forces in Nadia

Table-7 indicates that between 1961 and 1971, there has been a moderate increase in the percentage of male workers depending on agriculture; between 1941 and 1951, on the other hand, this percentage decrease significantly. The decreasing tendency was again observed in 1971-1981. Allied agricultural activities, e.g., involvement in fishing, plantation and orchard cultivation increased considerably between 1941 and 1961. Thereafter, the percentage of work-force absorbed in these sectors remained roughly unchanged as the percentage of male workers absorbed in the sector at various decennial points indicates. On the whole, the importance of agriculture and related activities seems to remain unchanged during the 40 years under consideration. Work-force absorption in industry including household industries increased slightly during 1941 and 1961, but the trend was slightly reversed during 1961-1971. In the last decade, it increased quite substantially. In other activities, except transport, no secular rise in the percentage of male work-force is indicated.

Considering all the non-agricultural activities excluding 'rural services' as urban activities[14], we rearrange the data of table-7 and construct table-8 which gives the decennial description of the percentage of male work-force in the urban activities. As the table suggests, 25.74 per cent of the total male work-force was engaged in urban activities in 1941. The percentage increased to 28.85 in 1951, indicating an 12.08 per cent increases in the percentage of male work-force in the urban activities.

This suggests that, compared to rural activities, the urban activities had better work-force absorption capacity during that period. A closer scrutiny of table-7 suggests that 'urban services' and 'trade and commerce' might have contributed largely to such a relative rise in the capacity of work force absorption in the urban sector. A drastic fall in the labour absorption in agriculture (largely due to migration of a large number of Muslim cultivators to East Pakistan without an immediate rehabilitation of immigrant Hindus in their lands) also contributed indirectly to such an urban tilt of the occupational pattern during this period.

However that be, what follows from table-8 is that during 1941-1951, urban activities had relatively higher potentiality of labour absorption so that it could attract or pull the population to the urban areas at a higher rate–a phenomenon which is adequately reflected in the pace of urbanisation during this period.

The relative importance of the urban sectors in terms of work-force absorption diminished during the next decade. The percentage of work-force in urban sector being 27.96 in 1961, one finds that compared to the position in 1951 there was a 3.08 per cent decline in the percentage of work-force in urban sectors. The decline was 5.51 per cent during the next decade. However, the 1981 census results show a significant acceleration (16.96 per cent) in the percentage of work force in urban sectors. Thus, between 1951 and

1971 the percentage of work-force in the urban activities declined by 9.19 per cent. This indicates that the urban activities lost the edge over rural activities during these two decades.

TABLE 7: **Percentage Distribution of the Male Work-force of the District (1941-81)**

Activities	1941(a)	1951	1961	1971	1981
Cultivation	68.23	44.87	45.15	38.85	32.96
Agricultural Labour		17.20	17.17	27.51	29.16
Allied Agricultural Activities (b)	4.69	3.42	3.40	2.88	2.93
Extractive Sector	0.00	neg.	0.15	0.02	0.02
Industry including Household	9.83	10.62	11.85	11.28	14.50
Construction	..	1.17	1.41	0.97	1.15
Transport	2.49	2.30	2.49	2.75	2.89
Trade & Commerce	8.34	11.36	7.53	7.41	8.53
Urban Services(c)	5.08	4.10	4.53	3.99	3.81
Rural Services	..	4.96	6.32	4.34	4.05
Others	1.38(d)				

(a) Excluding 'beggars and vagrants' and 'insufficiently described' persons.
(b) Allied agricultural activity means fishing, livestock raising, hunting, plantation and such other activities.
(c) Any service in the urban area.
(d) Includes 'person living on their own income' and 'domestic services'.

Sources: Means of Livelihood and Industries table, West Bengal (Y sample), Census 1941; Census of India 1951, Vol.VI, Part II; Census of India 1961, Vol.XVI, WB, Part II. A; Census of India 1971, Series 22. Pfart II A; Census of India 1981, Series 23, W.B., Part III. A and B (i).

TABLE 8: **Growth (decay) of work-force absorption in Urban sectors of Nadia (1941-81)**

	Per cent of workforce in urban activities (a)	Variation	Per cent variation in per cent of work-force in urban activities
1941	25.74	-	-
1951	29.55	+3.81	+14.80
1961	27.96	-1.59	-5.38
1971	26.42	-1.54	-5.51
1981	30.99	+4.57	+17.30

(a) For explanation, see footnote 13.
Source : Same as Table 7.

As a result, no 'urban pull' factor in terms of greater economic opportunities in the urban sector seems to have operated during this period. This might explain the virtual stagnation of urbanisation during these twenty years.

Several factors including decline in the percentage of work-force engaged in urban services and trade and commerce and virtual stagnation in industry including household during 1961 and 1971 are responsible for the relative decline of work-force in urban sectors. The work-force was tilted further to agriculture. More exactly, there had been a steady rise in the percentage of work-force absorbed as agricultural labourers.

The dwarfed growth of urban sector

As we gather from table-9, one feature of the urban development of Nadia is the excessive dependence of its urban work-force on tertiary activities like trade, commerce, transport and urban services. Thus, in 1951, 62.43 per cent of the urban work-force in Nadia depended on tertiary activities (Table 10(a)). The percentage declined during next three decades; but even then, the quantitative importance of such activities in still very high as the census data of 1961, 1971 and 1981 indicates.

Cultivation and allied activities, an element that brings a rural tilt in urban employment structure, also retains its importance. 9.27 per cent of the work-force was engaged in such an activity during 1951. Though the percentage decline to 4.90 in 1961; again it shot up to 12.05 per cent in 1971. The secular rise in the percentage of people engaged in agriculture as labourers is the most contributory factor for such a growing importance of agriculture in Nadia's urban areas. The percentage of agricultural labourers in the urban work-force recorded a 22.90 per cent decline during 1951-1961. However, at 1971, agricultural labourers accounted for 6.50 per cent of urban employment, thus denoting nearly a 300 per cent rise during 1961-1971 (Table 10(b)).

The role of industry and other related sectors generating non-agricultural material production, the core of urban economic activity, is not very important in the district. As table-10(a) indicates, employment in the secondary sector (Industry including household, Construction and Extractive Activities) did increase from 28.30 per cent during 1951-1961. But the tempo could not be maintained in the subsequent decade when the percentage of absorption of work-force in such sectors declined to 32.33. The urban development of Nadia thus retained the character of tertiary (and agriculture) led development during this period.

TABLE 9: **Percentage distribution of Male work-force in Urban Nadia (1951-1981)**

Activities	1951	1961	1971	1981
Cultivation	5.99	2.29	3.40	3.74
Agricultural Labour	2.35	1.65	6.50	6.70
Allied Agricultural activities	1.67	0.96	2.15	2.20
Extractive activities	negligible	0.04	0.06	0.05
Industry including household	23.62	28.47	29.17	36.49
Construction	4.18	4.32	3.10	2.60
Trade & Commerce	30.78	24.17	22.78	21.69
Transport	8.74	9.94	9.92	7.55
Services	22.67	28.16	22.92	19.03

Source : Same as Table 7.

TABLE 10(a): **Growth (decline) of work-force ifn various sectors in Urban Areas of Nadia**

Sectors	1951	1961	1971	1981
Agriculture:				
Cultivation & allied activities	7.13	3.25	5.55	5.94
Agricultural labourers	2.14	1.65	6.50	6.70
Industry & other material Production	28.30	32.83	32.33	39.12
Production of services (Tertiary)	62.43	62.27	55.62	48.24

Source: Ibid.

The inter census comparison of the distribution of work-force indicates (Table 10(b)) that during 1951-1961, there had been a remarkable shift of work-force towards industry largely (96.47) at the cost of primary activities. But the picture had changed during the next decade when there had been the shift of work-force not only from tertiary but also from secondary activities; the shifted work-force being absorbed largely in the primary (agriculture) sector, mainly (67.84 per cent) in the form of agricultural labourers.

As we have already noted, there had been a new spell of urbanisation in the district during 1971-1981. That this urbanisation was largely due to 'urban pull' factor is indicated by the fact that during 1971-1981, there had been a rise in the percentage of work-force absorbed in urban sector of Nadia (table-8, last row). The employment in the secondary sector increased; the percentage of urban work-force engaged in industry increased from 32.33 in 1971 to 39.72 in 1981. The overall domination of the tertiary sector prevailed. However, the percentage of urban work-force engaged in the tertiary declined from 55.62 to 48.24 (table 10(b)).

TABLE 10(b): **Measures of Variation**

Sectors	Percentate of total variation in the decade			Percentage rise or fall in the sector over previous decade		
	1951-61	1961-71	1971-81	1951-61	1961-71	1971-81
Agrirulture:						
Cultivation and allied activities	-85.65	+32.16	+5.28	-54.42	+70.77	+7.02
Agricultural labour	-10.82	+67.84	+2.71	-22.90	+293.93	+3.07
Industry & other material production	+100.00	-6.99	+92.01	+16.01	-1.52	+21.00
Production of Services (Tertiary)	-3.53	-93.01	-100.00	-0.26	-11.96	-15.27
Total:	100.00	100.00	100.00	-	-	-

Source: Ibid.

The demographic findings reported in this section may be summed up in the following way. In terms of the absorption of work-force, one finds that during 1951-1971 there was a decline in the relative position of the urban sector vis-a-vis the rural sector. This indicates that at least there was no 'urban pull' in the population movement which could induce migration from rural areas as voluntary response to greater economic opportunities in the urban areas. The inter-census comparison of the data indicates that such a relative stagnation or decay of the urban sector is largely explained by a secular decline in the relative employment potentiality in the tertiary sector, the largest employment generating sector in urban Nadia. Considering the pattern of the sectoral distribution of work force within urban Nadia, one observes that the nature of inter-sector movement of work-force was largely rural to urban during 1951-1961 in the sense that the decline of percentage of work force in primary activities in urban Nadia was largely counter balanced by a rise in the percentage of work-force in secondary activities. During

1961-1971, however, the character of the inter-sector movement of work-force was reversed. The percentage contribution declin in both services and secondary sectors, causing a push of population to agriculture, the rural activity, in the form of a conspicuous rise of the percentage of agricultural workers in urban areas. In a sense, this indicates that there had developed a 'push back' from urban sector in terms of the work-force absorbtion which discourage migration from rural areas, consequently the pace of urbanisation in the district was arrested. The tendency was reversed in 1971-1981 when the industrial employment registered a 21 per cent increase. The urban employment, however, still remained tertiary-oriented; 48.24 per cent of the work-force in urban Nadia is still employed in this sector.

Towards a Theory of Dwarfed Urbanisation

Contemporary economic theory on rural-urban migration is largely based on Lewis (1954) or Ranis and Fei (1961) type models of the reallocation of surplus rural labour through inter-sectoral population flows from agriculture or primary sector to industry; the wage differential depicting difference in marginal productivity is used as the key explanatory factor in such models. The apparently paradoxical situation of rising rural-urban migration in the context of rising unemployment in the urban areas is also taken care of in Harris and Todaro (1970) which postulates that 'migration proceeds in response to urban rural difference in expected earnings with the urban unemployment rate acting as an equilibrating force on such migration'.[15]

One would like to submit a sceptic note on the question of the analytical sufficiency of such models in the context of the economics of rural-urban migration and the pattern of urbanisation in the Third World countries. A model on migration and urbanisation with relative employment potentiality of the regions of emigration and urban rural difference in the expected or actual earnings as key explanatory factors is sensible. As theory, however, this is superficial; it is just a formalistion of the commonsense logic that the prospect of better economic opportunity is the major cause of every rational migration. Indeed, what else could be the apparent reason? A good theory, however, should go beyond such naivity and address itself to more complex questions; it should examine the factors that give rise to such differential employment prospects and the impact of such factors in the pattern of migration.

For example, consider the case of Nadia, the focus of attention in the present study. As we find, the pace of urbanisation in Nadia became poor, because the employment potentiality of urban Nadia had remained poor during the fifties and the sixties. This is quite a sensible observation and had we tried, we could fit a model of standard stock on the data. But we doubt the analytical robustness of such models because they formalise only a near obvious fact that a large scale rural-urban migration in the district had been discouraged due to the lack of a better economic prospect in urban Nadia. Is so much labour worthwhile simply for deriving such a superficial conclusion? What except the absence of better economic prospect be the immediate reason for the absence of large scale migration to urban Nadia? At the same time, how does such an observation help one grasp the real constraints of urban development in Nadia?

The last question becomes singularly important when one notes that there are indications in the census data that a meaningful study on the constraints of Nadia's urbanisation is possible if, instead of concentrating on such a near obvious explanatory factor, viz., the employment opportunity in urban areas, one probes deeper into the problem and considers the structure of employment generating activities in urban Nadia and the factors that shape the trend of the dominant element or elements of the structure. Let us elucidate this point with the help of the data we have already presented.

Considering the structure of the employment generating activities in urban Nadia, it has been observed that the structure is heavily biased in favour of tertiary activities; evidence from various census data establish this point unequivocally. There are also evidences in support of the contention that the dominant element of the structure of employment generating activities, i.e., the tertiary sector recorded a poor progress over time in terms of absorption of work force. Logically speaking, the dwarfed growth of tertiary activities could, therefore, be considered as an important causal factor behind the poor expansion of urban employment in Nadia.

If we consider now the factors that shape the trend of the dominant element of the structure of urban employment, i.e., if we consider factors behind such a poor growth of tertiary activities, a meaningful explanation of dwarfed urbanisation could be developed in the following way. The growth of tertiary activities being a function of the growth of productive activities in primary and secondary sectors, a town with excessive dependence on the tertiary activities for generation of employment makes its economy a mere adjunct to the metropolitan and the adjacent rural economics, which produce secondary and primary commodities, respectively. The independent growth potentiality being absent, the level of urban development or non-development of these urban centres is thus determined by some factors which are exogeneous to these urban centres. With a poor growth of agriculture in the rural hinterlands and a stangnating industry in the nearby metropolis, the tertiary activities in these centres are bound to register a dwarfed growth and consequently the pace of urbanisation is likely to remain poor. Our understanding is that a model developed on this line fits well to the empirical exercise that we have developed in this paper. With a moderate percentage of the work-force in the manufacturing sector of Nadia, limits to Nadia's urbanisation had been set by the poor expansion of the tertiary sector. The poor rate of expansion of tertiary sector is again explained by the poor pace of industrialisation in Calcutta urban conglomerate[16] and a not-so-good performance of Nadia's agriculture.[17]

Nadia's experience lays bare the weakness of a 'tertiary led' urban growth programme. It should be noted that the stagnation and the decay of the old towns and poor pace of urbanisations, as we find in case of Nadia, are not some exceptional observations. Also, the domination and the dwarfed growth of tertiary activities in urban centres are not unique to urban Nadia. With a poor pace of industrialisation, and a perpetual backwardness in agriculture, such things are expected to occur in most of the semi-feudal and semi-colonial countries of the Third World. It is our understanding that Lewis (1954), Ranis-Fei(1961) or Harris-Todaro (1970) type models fail to capture the intricate economic rationale of such developments. Such phenomena should, therefore, receive more attention from the demographers and the economists.

NOTES

1. The term 'urban' has been used in the paper in a restricted sense. It adheres to the census definition of 'town' as adopted in 1951 census of West Bengal (which has subsequently been accepted as standard definition all over India since 1961); (A. Mitra (1980) p. XVII).

2. By 'rate of urban growth' we mean the per cent increase in the urban population in a given decade.
3. By 'rate of urbanisation' we mean the per cent increase in the proportion of the urban population to the total population during a given decade.
4. Nadia covers only 4.46 per cent of the total geographical area of the State. According to 1971 census, the population of Nadia is about 5.00 per cent of the total population of West Bengal.
5. We are considering only that part of erstwhile Nadia of undivided Bengal which now belongs to India.
6. Bose (1974), page 59.
7. *Utbandi* is a type of tenurial arrangement under which "the holding is not fixed either in area or in position but consists of a variable parcel or parcels of land ascertained by measurement or inspection made at least once a year. The rent is paid for each year or season in respect of the parcel or parcels of land which has been ascertained by the said measurement or inspection" (as quoted in District Gazetteers, Nadia (1978), page 291). *Utbandi* had been the prevalent form of tenurial arrangement in Kaliganj, Nakasipara, Nabadwip, Krishnanagar and Santipur regions of the district.
8. The Cholera epidemic of 1902-1908 and Influenza epidemic of this period.
9. According to Census 1951, total migration to Nadia had been 464462, of which 426907 had been displaced persons from East Pakistan, the rest being intra-state immigrants. The estimated emigration from the district (of the Muslim population to East Pakistan) being about 120,000, the net inflow to the district comes to 344462 persons, net inflow from East Pakistan being 306907 persons.
10. Taken together, these towns accounted for 98 per cent, 95 per cent and more than 80 per cent of total urban population of the district in 1941, 1951 and 1971 respectivity.
11. As mentioned in Mitra, A. (1953) from the Settlement Report, 1918-26.
12. Immigration as percentage of the total population had been 0.95 and 0.83 in 1921 and 1931 respectively (compiled from District Census, 1921 and 1931).
13. Of course, this is not a census category. Any 'service' (as defined by census) in the urban area has been assumed to belong to such a category.
14. 'Urban activities' do not necessarily mean activities in the urban areas. These are activities like Extraction, Household and Non-household Manufacture, Construction, Trade, Transport and Urban Services. However, the urban percentage of the male work-force in those sectors is substantially high in Nadia (see District Census Handbook, 1971).
15. Harris & Todaro (1970). Quoted here from Todaro (1976).
16. For a study on the industrial stagnation with special reference to West Bengal, see Banerjee, Debdas (1982). This gives an idea about recent stagnation in industrial activities in Calcutta urban conglomerate because most of industrial activities of the state is concentrated near Calcutta.
17. Compared to other districts of the state, Nadia's performance in agriculture is moderate. Thus, in terms of the index of agricultural production, Nadia ranked 5th during 1979-1980. HYV crops as percentage of gross cropped areas was just 13.04 per cent in 1974-1975, the rank being the 6th. The rank of the district in terms of the non-traditional irrigation as percentage of gross cropped area was 7th during 1976-77. For a detailed study, see Khasnabis, R. and Chakravarty, J. (1982).

REFERENCES

1. Banerjee, Debdas: Industrial Stagnation in Eastern India - A Statistical Investigation, *Economic and Political Weekly*, Feb. 20 and Feb. 27, 1982.
2. Bose, A.: Urban Growth and Urbanisation in India : 1901-1971, *Tata McGraw Hill*, New Delhi, 1974.
3. Government of West Bengal : Census 1941, Means of Livelihood Tables, West Bengal (Y-Sample).
   - District Census Handbook, Nadia, 1951, 1961, 1971.
   - District Gazetteers of Nadia, 1978, State Statistical Bureau.
   - Report on the Sample Survey for Estimating the Socio-economic Characteristics of Displaced Persons Migrating from Eastern Pakistan to the State of West Bengal, Calcutta, 1951 (a).
   - State Statistical Bureau, Rehabilitation of Refugees : A Statistical Survey, 1955, Calcutta; 1956.
4. Harris, J.R. and Tadaro, M.P. : Migration, Unemployment and Development : A Two Sector Analysis, *The American Economic* Review, LX, I. 1970.
5. Khasnabis, R. and Chakrabarty, J. : Mode of Surplus Utilisation in West Bengal Agriculture : Nadia District - A case study, *Unpublished report*, 1982; Chapter 1 of this volume.
6. Lewis, A. : Economic Development with Unlimited Supply of Labour, *Manchester School of Economic and Social Studies* XXII (1954).
7. Mitra, A. : An Account of Land Management in West Bengal (1850-1950), *Government of West Bengal*, 1953.
8. Mitra, A. and Others : Population and Area of Cities Towns and Urban Agglomerations, 1872-1971, Allied, 1980.
9. Ranis, G. and Fei, J.C.H. : A Theory of Economic Development, *The American Economic Review*, LI, 3, 1961.
10. Tadoro, M.P. : Rural-Urban Migration, Unemployment and Job probabilities : Recent Theoretical and Empirical Research, in *Economic Factors in Population Growth*, Edited by A.J. Coale *Macmillan Press*, 1976.

This chapter was prepared in collaboration with Nirmalendu Nath.

APPENDIX III

LIST OF HOUSEHOLDS VISITED

Sl. No.	Name of Respondent	Village (With J.L.[1] No.)
Block : Haringatha		
1.	Rabi Kumar Sarkar	Sat Simulia, Chowberia (31)
2.	Ismail Miah	Sonakur, Amin Kandia (80)
3.	Pramathanath Mondal (Rajen Mondal)	Sat Simulia (31)
Block : Chakdah		
4.	Kanai Mondal	Mandalhat Ghata Gachi (137)
5.	Banamali Ghosh	Khorgacchi Rantari (115)
6.	Panchu Gopal Ghosh	Saguna (80) (P.S. Kalyani)
7.	Birendra Nath Datta	Deuli (187)
8.	Nani Bhandari	Jaguli (138)
9.	Anwar Hossin	Belgaria (127)
Block : Ranaghat I		
10.	Santibhusan Biswas	Doharpur (6)
11.	Mangalmay Ghosh	Majdia, Maynapara Andulia (125)
12.	Binay Kr. Chatterjee	Ranaghat School Lane Ranaghat (155)

---

1. Jurisdiction List Number of the Settlement Circle Office.

13.	Tarapada Paul (Dead) (Respondent : Wife)	Hajrapur (35)
14.	Gayaram Mondal	Bhadurua (2)
15.	Kamal Prasanna Sarkar	Taherpur Natunpara (4)
16.	Harinaranyan Ray	Habibpur (116)
17.	Bishnupada Pramanik	Asutoshpur (114)

Block: Hanskhali

18.	Bihdubasini Biswas W/o Late Ramesh ch. Biswas	Gajna (18)
19.	Gourpada Biswas	Fatepur (21)
20.	Nani Ghosh	Fatepur (21)
21.	Dulal Chandra Haldar	Betna (6)
22.	Kalipada Sarkar	Badkulla (44)
23.	Panchu Gopal Ghosh	Badkulla (44)
24.	Nalinikanta Joardar	Badkulla (44)
25.	Ashim Kr. Sarkar	Badkulla (44)
26.	Nilpada Ghosh	Silberia (78)
27.	Hazi Ml. Rabin Box Mondal	Silberia (78)
28.	Santosh Kr. Gan	Pipulberia (19)
29.	Rasik Lal Roy	Bhaina (67)
30.	Murari Ghosh	Gobindapore (33)
31.	Dinabandhu Biswas	Sanatanpore (24)
32.	Bijoy Krishna Gan	Majdia, Krishnaganj (59)
33.	Birendranath Bhattacharyya	Dhakuria (4)
34.	Brajabala Ghosh	Dosotina (46)
35.	Harendranath Ghosh S/o Harish Chandra Ghosh	Gajna (18)
36.	Nityananda Biswas	Bhairab Chandrapore (10)
37.	Samit Biswas	Badkulla (44)
38.	Anil Kr. Biswas	Gayes (56)
39.	Ajit Ghosh	Fatepur (21)
40.	Hasi Rakshit	Shyamnagar (82)

Block : Santipur

41.	Umapada Mondal	Karanchaputti Bayachra (29)
42.	Indu Bhusan Banerjee	Rathala Santipur (22)
43.	Indulekha Devi	Nrisingapore Santipur Fulia (16)

44.	Brajen Dewan S/o Nalin Dewan	Arbandhi (66)
45.	Kalicharan Mondal (Dead) Nemai Ghosh (heir)	Bansdob (63)
46.	Suresh Chandra Ghosh	Baincha Fulia (70)
47.	Deben Biswas	Lalmath (57)
48.	Chaitanya Mondal	Char Ramnagar (81)
49.	Alam Shah	Bagdia (34)
50.	Pramathanath Ghosh	Simulia (77)
51.	Birendranath Sarkar	Chuttkutula (44)
52.	Naresh Biswas	(Natun) Phulia (54)

Block : Ranaghat II

53.	Dastu Md. Mondal	Hajripur (35)
54.	Nagendra Nath Biswas	Hosenpur, Aranghata (51)
55.	Baidya Ranjan Tarafder	Purbanapore (91)
56.	Aswini Kr. Mondal	Petua, Aranghata (47)
57.	Satya Charan Chakraborty	Bankimnagar Hijuli (112)
58.	Birendra Nath Biswas	Patuli, Beyopara (151)
59.	Nirmal Chandra Biswas	Patuli, Beyopara (151)
60.	Paritosh Ghosh	Purbanoapara (73)
61.	Dhirendra Nath Ghosh	Purananawapara (73)
62.	Pratima Rani Mitra	Eruli (98)
63.	Bhiswadev Biswas	Hosenpur, Aranghata (51)
64.	Ranibala Ghosh (Dead) W/o Gour Chandra Ghosh (Respondent)	Raynagore Naserkuli (161)
65.	Suresh Banerjee (heir) Nalini Chatterjee (Dead)	Muragachha Chhotto Bazar (171)
66.	Surendranath Kundu	Matikumra (108)
67.	Bibhuti Bhusan Biswas	Nokari (160)
68.	Ranajit Kr. Roy	Dhautola (67)
69.	Surendra Nath Kundu	Matikumra (108)
70.	Panchannan Ghosh	Gangnapur (North) (175)

Block : Kaliganj

71.	Abu Taher Mondal	Basarkhola (56)
72.	Khagendranath Chattopadhyay	Molanodi (121)
73.	Kanan Kumar Dey	Kaliganj (18)

Block : Nakasipara

74.	Biswanath Mukho padhyay	Chichuria (42)
75.	Kashinath Singha Roy	Sonadanga (23)
76.	Saiyad Mondal	Birpur (87)
77.	Gopal Das Ghosh	Dadupur (61)
78.	Dhirendranath Ghosh	Dogachhia (97)
79.	Prafulla Chandra Sikdar	Nakasipara (54)
80.	Manmatha Nath Sarkar	Dhaparia (83)
81.	Nemai Chandra Mondal- (Heir) Tarini Mondal (Dead)	Uday Chandrapur (60)
82.	Saktipada Pramanik	Nutan Gotpara (58)
83.	Umapada Ray	Nangla (67)
84.	Japhar Ali Sheikh	Haridapotta (106)
85.	Narayan Chandra Chatterjee	Bekoail (79)
86.	Meher Ali Sheikh	Kanthal-baria (47)
87.	Bimal Mondal	Uttar Bahirgachhi (37)

Block : Krishnanagar -I

88.	Anada Rani Biswas W/o Late Panchu Gopal Biswas	Jahangirpur (88)
89.	Tarapada Garai	Chandpur (c)[2] (93)
90.	Nivanani Biswas	Bhimpur (c) (91)
91.	Anil Kumar Ghosh	Tetia Kotoali (86)
92.	Sudhendu Kr. Banerjee	Arshihari (98)

Block : Krishnagar - II

93.	Mela Bibi W/o Late- Doud Mondal	Pukuria (43)
94.	Samsuddin Ahmed	Rukunpur (1)

Block : Tehatta - I

95.	Rabindranath Biswas	Dhopahat (28)
96.	Bhaktaram Biswas	Kustia (34)
97.	Dilip Kr. Ghosal (Adhikari)	Bahadurpur (70)
98.	Rabi Dutta	Tehatta (101)
99.	Santosh Singha Ray	Kustia (34)

---

2. J.L. Nos. with affix (c) denote villages from P.S. Chopra of Nadia District transferred to Krishnanagar dated 8.1.66

Block : Tehatta - II

100.	Saffatullah Mondal	Palsunda (14)
101.	Phaniy Bushan Joardar	Radhanagar (45)
102.	Kinkar Kr. Biswas (Indumati Dasi) (W/o Jyotindranath Biswas)	Hanspurkuria (35)
103.	Adyanath Mondal	Barnia (26)
104.	Kartik Channdra Biswas	Sahebnagar (18)
105.	Kazi Nazrul Islam	Palsunda (14)
106.	Samsul Haq	Palsunda (14)
107.	Nani Gopal Sarkar	Chhotto Naldaha (17)
108.	Jamini Ranjan Mondal	Sahebnagar (18)
109.	Jyotindra Mohan - Biswas	Abhayanagar (9)
110.	Purna Chandra Mondal	Chhotto Naldaha (17)

Block : Karimpur

111.	Niranjan Sarkar (Ramapratap Chatto padhyay S/o Saradanat Chottopadhyay Salkia,Howrah)	Karimpur (6)
112.	Hemlata Biswas W/o Ramanimohan Biswas	Daskhin Gopalpore (32)
113.	Aditya Kumar Ghosh	Thanapara (37)
114.	Amarendra Biswas	Natna (36)
115.	Arun Kr. Maitra	Natidanga (14)
116.	Nityagopal Dey	Narayanpore (21)
117.	Mahit Ram Mondal	Kantalia (55)
118.	Gobinda Chandra Ghosh	Daiwanpara Swapanpur (10)
119.	Harendranath Sarkar	Natna (86)

Block : Chapra

120.	Basanta Ghosh	Tengra (81)
121.	Narayan Ch. Singha	Bara Andulia (3)
122.	Arshad Biswas	Kukradoha (74)
123.	Kamala Bala Dasi W/o Naba Ghosh	Kultala (82)
124.	Dulal Ghosh	Mahespore (79)
125.	Phulkumari Biswas W/o Late Panchu Gopal Biswas	Pipragachhi (62)
126.	Dilip Dutta	Arangsarisha (41)
127.	Binay Bhushan Biswas	Pipragachhi (62)

128.	Balai Ghosh	Katgara (68)
129.	Ranajay Singha Roy	Hatisala (1)
130.	Aloke Kumar Biswas	Dair Bazar (91)

Block : Nabadwip

131.	Chandrakanta Ghosh	Gadkhaly (28)
132.	Bhaktachandra Ghosh	Idrakpore (Mayapore) (1)
133.	Ranjit Ghosh	Idrakpur (1)
134.	Ranjit Kr. Paul	Kalinagar (23)

Block : Krishnaganj

135.	Shibprasad Roychowdury	Pabakhali (60)
136.	Sudhir Kr. Biswas	Joyghata (8)
137.	Shambhu Charan Ghosh	Bishnupore (3)
138.	Bhadrayaswar Mondal	Mathurapur (42)

INDEX